James MacDonell

France since the First Empire

James MacDonell

France since the First Empire

ISBN/EAN: 9783744727556

Printed in Europe, USA, Canada, Australia, Japan

Cover: Foto ©ninafisch / pixelio.de

More available books at **www.hansebooks.com**

FRANCE

SINCE THE FIRST EMPIRE

BY

JAMES MACDONELL

EDITED BY HIS WIFE.

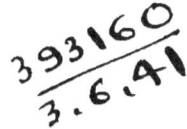

London:
MACMILLAN AND CO.
1879.

The Right of Translation is reserved.

CHARLES DICKENS AND EVANS,
CRYSTAL PALACE PRESS.

PREFACE.

It seems necessary to say a few words to explain how this book was written. I am conscious that it is not what it would have been had my husband lived to finish it.

He meant it to be a complete history of the different parties, which for centuries in France have struggled and fought, each one in turn gaining supreme power by trampling the others under foot, and which still represent political life and feeling in France.

He loved France with an ardent love. He longed to make his countrymen just to her, to make them understand her history and sympathise with her difficulties. He studied her history and her literature with ceaseless interest. Newspapers, essays, memoirs, histories were carefully read, and from them were volumes of notes taken. The time, however, which he could give to this beloved work was but scanty, and probably many years would have passed, had he lived, before the book could have been finished. One chapter only, "Revival of the Legitimist Monarchy," has that finish which he ever strove should be in all which he gave to the public. The other chapters lack the completeness he meant they should have, but I send them out as they were left by him.

My husband's intention was to describe fully the four great parties which govern France: the Legitimist, the Orleanist, the Bonapartist, and the Republican. Only the first three of these find their place in this volume. The chapters devoted to the Republican party were to have been the most important in the book. In this party my husband felt the keenest interest, and the description of its sufferings and its victories, its hopes and its fears, its past and its future, would have filled more than half the book, and would have been written only after many months of careful reading. The writing of this portion was never even begun. I have a volume of notes—all that is left of countless hours of patient study, and of conscientious research!

The last chapter, however, gives an account of the present position of the Republic. This chapter

I owe to the kindness of my husband's much-prized friend, Mr. Meredith Townsend. I am very glad to have this opportunity of saying how grateful I feel to Mr. Townsend and the other friends who have so freely given me help.

Something else I must mention. The labour of this book was done in my husband's leisure hours. He was a journalist. And no man was prouder of his profession, no man ever strove harder to put his conscience into all that he did. His indefatigable energy never ceased. In the years that we were together, I know that this untiring zeal never relaxed. Personal comfort, pleasure, health, all were disregarded until the full claims of his professional duties had been fulfilled.

In spite, however, of the exhausting labours of his profession—and journalists alone know what they are—he managed to put together the materials of this book, a fragment merely, I sadly feel, of what it was meant to be.

ANNIE H. MACDONELL.

BECKENHAM: *November*, 1879.

CONTENTS.

CHAPTER I.
ENGLISH INTEREST IN FRENCH POLITICS   1

CHAPTER II.
REVOLUTIONARY CAUSES OF DISPEACE   6

CHAPTER III.
THE POLITICAL TENDENCIES OF THE CATHOLIC CHURCH... 34

CHAPTER IV.
THE CLERICAL PARTY 52

CHAPTER V.
REVIVAL OF THE LEGITIMIST MONARCHY 92

CHAPTER VI.
THE LEGITIMISTS 156

CHAPTER VII.
THE ORLEANISTS 164

CHAPTER VIII.
BONAPARTISTS 226

CHAPTER IX.
THE BONAPARTISTS 275

THE REPUBLIC 295

FRANCE SINCE THE FIRST EMPIRE.

CHAPTER I.

ENGLISH INTEREST IN FRENCH POLITICS.

IF the French like the flattery of attention, they have good reason to be pleased by the notice which they get from England, in their darkest as in their brightest years. Sedan, the Commune, the loss of Alsace and Lorraine, and the payment of the indemnity to Germany seemed, for a moment, to strike their country from the list of Great Powers, and, at any rate, those events made the sceptre of political power pass beyond the Rhine; yet none the less did the English people continue to think and read a hundred times more about Paris than Berlin.

Our newspapers followed all the windings in the long strife which was closed by the establishment of the Republic. The attempts of the Legitimists and the Orleanists to bring about a fusion, in which they should put the accusing memories of 1830 out of sight for the sake of overthrowing their common enemy the Republic; their long strifes with M. Thiers; their dismissal of that statesman and their choice of Marshal MacMahon; the quick passage of the Duc de Broglie, M. Buffet, and M. de Fourtou across the field of intrigue; the restraining and guiding influence of M. Gambetta; the establishment of the Republic by its enemies; the last desperate effort of Royalists, Bonapartists, and Clericals to entrust the citadel of power to the sworn foes of the constitution; the defeat of that scheme by the union of peasant with artisan votes —all that tangled story was told by our chief journals with at least as much minuteness as the less exciting narrative of our own domestic history. Even the danger and excitement of the war between Russia and Turkey failed to draw English eyes away from the battle between parliamentary and personal forces in France. M. Thiers, Marshal MacMahon, Duc de Broglie, M. de Fourtou, M. Buffet, and M. Gambetta are at least as vivid figures to Englishmen as the secondary personages of our own Parliament.

The general wish to watch the political life of France comes partly from the charm which has been cast over civilised mankind by her grand and tragic history, by the brilliancy of her literature, the fascination of her manners, and the rich store of graces which lift her above the prose of life. Partly, it is a tribute to the interest of national calamity. Partly, it springs from the anticipation of some new and great change in a history which has been already seamed with revolutions. Partly, it is the fruit of the dulness which has settled in the domestic policy of our own country. Satire has said that the only thing which all the members of the

Liberal party have heartily agreed to support is Mr. Osborne Morgan's Burials Bill. But it is not very easy even for the most conscientious Liberal to spend all his enthusiasm on the right of Dissenters to bury each other without the aid of a surplice and the Prayer-book. Political excitement must be sought elsewhere when the domestic affairs of England do not rise above the sedate respectability of a select vestry. Hence we naturally look to the more troubled field of France, because she is still a country of unsolved political problems which go down to the roots of government, religious convictions, and society. She has more open questions than any other land, and she often handles them with a logical fearlessness which, if sometimes fatal to her governments, is profoundly instructive to all political students. For eighty years she has been the great field of experiments in the art of shaping and ruling society.

The tissues of the national life have been laid bare by the surgery of revolution, so that the diseases of civilised communities and their sources of vigour may be more clearly seen in her annals than in those of any other country. She has repeated, in larger form, some of the perils through which we have passed; she has also foreshadowed, perhaps, the dangers which we may have to meet in no distant future. Her history is a magnifying mirror in which we may see a lesson and a prophecy. The best way to profit by both reflections is to glance at her political and religious parties, and to trace the parentage of each even at the cost of going over some well-worn scenes of history.

CHAPTER II.

REVOLUTIONARY CAUSES OF DISPEACE.

LET anyone go into the Chamber of Deputies at Versailles during a stormy debate, and he will get a more vivid idea of the profound differences of opinion, and the implacable hates which have tossed France from one revolution to another, than he would obtain from volumes of philosophical analysis. The scene—which has been so often described that I need not repeat the picture—may appear to be a satire on representative government. When Republicans insinuate that the Royalists are priest-ridden or hypocritical, and that the Bonapartists are a gang of unconvicted criminals; when Royalists and Imperialists insinuate that the Republicans are Communards at heart, and responsible for the massacre of the hostages; when such invectives awaken a tempest of interruption which the president's bell and threats cannot still, and when he can sometimes restore order only by stopping the business of the day, the nation might appear to be on the brink of civil war.

Such is the Chamber of Deputies and such is France. In her parliament we see the picture of the discords which have made her the sport of revolution for eighty years. We see, not one France, but several Frances, each unable to live at peace beside the others.

Englishmen usually explain such outbursts of temper, such discordant aims, such a tendency to seek refuge in barricades and military conspiracies, by a theory which flatters their national pride. The French, it is said, are flighty and fickle; always rushing from one extreme to another; and, as they never know when they are well off, the only way to keep them quiet is to keep them down.

A Frenchman might, however, recall some passages in our own history which suggest that Englishmen do not always confine their words or their conduct within the bounds of dignified repose. Some of the scenes in the Long Parliament were as stormy as any in the recent National Assemblies of France. Even in our own decorous days, when the House of Commons is agitated by no controversies of high moment, the noise and the temper of both sides have sometimes been qualified as scandalous. The truth is, that the decorum in our own House of Commons springs in great part from the dulness of our political existence. We fight about none of the things which go down to the roots of a nation's life. The monarchy and religion are as much beyond the pale of parliamentary discussion as if they were in the moon. But they were not always fixed in such serenity. Frenchmen may well marvel at the complacency with which we lecture their country on its turbulence, when they call to mind how prone we were to revolutionary courses while they were the quietest, the most loyal, and the most stable nation in Europe. The French were once as peaceful as we are now, and we were once almost as turbulent as they are to-day. Somewhat more than a hundred years elapsed between the quarrel of Charles I. with the Long Parliament and the battle of Culloden; and during all that time the history of quiet, respectable, money-making, religious, stable England is the history of revolution, civil war, plots at the court, dynastic intrigue, popular violence, and foreign invasion. A king was beheaded and the throne overturned. A republic was set up, and the chief power fell into the hands of a man whose consummate practical genius included all the highest gifts of the soldier, the prince, and the statesman. We had a restoration with which the Restoration of France need fear no comparison. Another king was sent into exile. The treachery of trusted statesmen nearly led to another restoration; and the second of two Jacobite rebellions did not seem to be very far from the brink of triumph.

It took us a hundred years to find calm after our own small revolution; and yet we are the most practical nation on the face of the earth. And what was the cause of all our troubles? It was the agitation of the English mind by two hostile, profound, and incalculably important convictions, which seemed to admit of no compromise. Men believed, on the one hand, that the prerogatives of a court and a sacerdotal church were worth dying for. Men believed, on the other, that without civil and religious freedom life was not worth having. For the moment, we have practically solved these fundamental differences of opinion. Fighting about little more than details, we are now able to lead a quiet life.

Such facts might suffice to silence some of the easy moralising on the fickleness of France. She has not yet taken so long to recover from the tremendous shock of her Revolution as we took to repair the comparatively feeble violence of ours. It is probable, however, that she has still to reach a day of peace. It would be no wonder, indeed, if she should be disturbed for another generation by the subsiding waves of the most tremendous political storm that ever broke over modern society. We have had no experience of the misrule and the misery, the savage discontent and the wild remedial theories, which were the heralds of their revolution. Partly, it is true, those evils may be connected with some organic weakness in the character of the French people themselves; and the root of that weakness can be removed, perhaps, by nothing but the surgery of experience. Another cause of the calamities may be found in the fact that, as a continental state, France was always open to invasion; that she needed a standing army at an early period of her history, and that the court was thus able to crush both feudal and municipal freedom. Not less important was the fact that a military court was able to throw its weight into the scale of Catholicism, at a time when Protestantism seemed to have a fairer prospect than in any other part of Europe; when it was drawing to its side the flower both of the common people and of the nobility, and when a spirit of national devotion was thus preparing a safe outlet both for religious enthusiasm and critical inquiry. The Revolution was calamitous also because the most Catholic and profligate of courts was thus able to destroy the best of the middle class and the most powerful barrier against the violence of mobs and soldiers. The Catholicism of Louis XIV. and his Jesuit confessors had, by revoking the Edict of Nantes, left France no Puritanism. Thus, on the eve of the Revolution, the frivolity of the nobles, the extravagance of the court, the slavishness of the Church to the king and his ministers, the misery of the people, the discontent, and the Utopian theories of reform made up a scene of social anarchy, to which there is no parallel in the troubles preceding the rise of our own Commonwealth. A great convulsion was inevitable. Unless the French had been made of more seraphic stuff than common mortals, it was impossible for the Revolution to be effected without terrible calamities and crimes. M. Taine's book, "Les Origines de la France Contemporaine," gives a masterly and merciless picture of the follies, the blunders, the charlatanism and the villainy of the revolutionists; but it is an indictment of human nature rather than of his own countrymen. Nor has anyone been able to point out how the torrent could have been stopped by such resources as lie at the command of statesmanship. It is sometimes said that everything might have been changed, if the court had given its confidence to Mirabeau at the outset of the struggle, if Mirabeau had lived a little longer, or if the king had taken his advice by leaving Paris immediately after he was brought from Versailles. But it is little short of ridiculous to believe that such petty expedients could have materially broken the force of the storm. Mirabeau's correspondence shows that even he had not correctly measured the tremendous power of the passions which had been let loose. He had to fight against the passions, not merely of the inexperienced crowd, but of kings, courts, nobles, soldiers, and priests, who, in all parts of the Continent, thought that there would be an end of political Europe if the enemies of the king should succeed. We may see how helpless was mere routine statesmanship at such a crisis if we look at the career of the Girondists. Those men were the Whigs of France. They had so far formed a true idea of political progress, as to see that they must not cut the historic thread of the national life on pain of bringing on a great convulsion. They dimly saw that the moss of tradition and sentiment and religious faith, which gathers round an historic monarchy, cannot be removed by a parliamentary decree : that a republic could not be made without republicans, and that republicans could not be manufactured by law. They dimly saw, in fact, that to retain the throne in some modified form would be better for the cause of progress, than to try the experiment of a commonwealth.

They themselves would gladly have been moderate. But the monarchy had a set of friends to whom all the democratic work was bad and impious; who believed that the elements of the revolt might have been kept in hand, if the king had never yielded an inch to the clamour of reform; and who thought that there was still time to win back by swift peremptory force of steel the old rights of the court, the nobles, and the Church. Hence, Radical reformers saw everywhere signs of plots against the Revolution; plots at the court, plots in the Church, plots among the nobles. They were quite right; such plots did exist, and must have existed. Thus, the Radical reformers said that they were fighting with halters round their necks, and that, if they did not put down the king's party, the king's party would put down them. Again they were perfectly right. The Comte d'Artois and the leaders of the foreign armies would have been miracles of forbearance if, in the event of a victory over the enemies of the throne, they had not dealt out signal vengeance among a set of men whom they thought, and must have thought, worse than the worst of criminals. The dainty distinction between criminal and political offences is good for quiet times; but how little it stands the strain of civil strife, even in our own philanthropic days, we may see from the way in which M. Thiers and the Royalists put down the Commune and punished its defenders. Thus, there was real practical logic in the cry of the Mountain that they must tie the hands of the court and the aristocracy. Girondists could not resist that cry without seeming to be traitors, and perhaps they spoke more vehemently than they felt in order to answer the imputations cast on their own sincerity. Hence, they joined in the howl against the sovereign. It is melancholy to think that the most passionate as well as eloquent speeches against the king came from Vergniaud. Thus were the moderate Liberals hurried with the stream of terror and ferocity which was to cover the Republic with infamy.

They no doubt repented before the end. When they saw that they had gone too far; when old champions of the Mountain like Camille Desmoulins came forward to denounce the prevailing reign of ferocity; when Danton himself turned away from the work of butchery like one sick of life—the Girondists chose to die rather than submit any longer to the hideous authority which they had helped to create. But it was then too late; they themselves were already doomed, and the Republic was doomed too. And yet, I repeat, it is impossible to see the exact point at which the descent from reform to crime and ruin could have been stopped. Whole masses of men seemed to be the sport of a dark fate, which drove them blindly and helplessly to destruction. No series of events in modern history would appear to have been so little capable of management by any one man or group of men.

To do such men as Robespierre justice, it must be admitted that they set less store by the safety of their own necks than by the good of the Republic. They looked on the Republic with a species of religious ecstasy. Democracy had given them a kind of spiritual creed—the only faith suitable for minds which had been nourished by the gospel of Rousseau and the apologetics of Diderot. Still greater enthusiasm perhaps did the declaration of the rights of man, and the institution of the Republic, excite among the unlettered crowds who nightly filled the Jacobin and the Cordelier clubs. They really seemed to believe that the abolition of the throne and the banishment of the nobles, the destruction of the Church, the institution of legal equality, and the general triumph of democracy would heal half the evils of humanity. The hard eternal realities of life—poverty, pain, and sorrow, bad passions, the misery which men make for themselves, and which renders them slaves—seem to fly away into some dark dreamland of the past, in the midst of eloquent talk. Much of that vision began and ended no doubt with the moment of oratorical excitement; much of the accompanying oratory was purely artificial; some of it must have been mendacious; and in time the grim experience of depreciated paper money and dear bread chilled the enthusiasm awakened by the gospel of democracy. But there remained a real, intense, fanatical, aggressive faith in the power of the Republic to heal the woes of France and of mankind. Justice cannot be done to the chiefs of the Revolution if we do not bear in mind that they saw, in its principles and practice, the beginning of a new time for this heavy-laden earth. It was the fanatical strength of that belief which made them ruthless. Robespierre was a priggish country lawyer, puritanical in language and even in conduct. Danton had many virtues as well as vices. Even Marat, the most repulsive of the whole band, might, if cast in quieter times and employed in some petty sect or parochial legislature, have been enabled to escape any worse reproach than that of being a self-conceited and intolerable bore. All the scoundrelism of France, as well as all the enthusiasm, was placed at the service of the Revolution. Rascality always comes to the surface in moments of sudden, even if beneficent, change.

Notwithstanding all the crimes of the Revolution, it did bring a new time to the common people. By freeing the land from the burden of feudal dues and multiplying the number of small cultivators, it did more than any other act in the history of any nation to lift the peasantry above the curse of poverty. That result was, no doubt, but the natural close of a tendency which existed long before 1789, and the sources of which must be sought in the twilight of French history.

The French peasant has for centuries had a passionate desire to get possession of the little piece of land which he has tilled. Hence he pinched and hoarded during the most miserable periods of a history which for him was never bright. Thus great portions of the land passed into his keeping, in spite of hardships which seem to cast the very shadow of death over the annals of the most brilliant and the gayest of nations; in spite of tax-gatherers by whom, to use the Hebrew metaphor, the people were eaten as though they were bread; in spite of pestilence and famine; in spite of all the evils which promise to live in the vivid memory of the latest generations of Frenchmen. It is astonishing to find the amount of land which had passed to the peasantry, before the Revolution came to deliver them from the bondage of feudal exactions. Thus in the country districts of France the course of the poor people was precisely the opposite of what it was in England. In France they went towards the land; in England they went away from it. And the Revolution did but express the general tendency of the nation when it provided that the property of each person should, after his death, be divided amongst his heirs in nearly equal portions, and that he should possess freedom of bequest only over one share. The law expressed a still profounder tendency of the French mind, and that was a passion for equality. At one time the French people may have been as fond of an aristocracy as our own people are of theirs; but the behaviour of the French nobles cured them of that passion. Causes which I cannot stop to point out made the nobles gradually neglect those feudal duties which, at one period, were the service done in return for feudal dues. They went to court and wasted their money in the gaieties of Versailles. When they lived on their estates, they spent their time in hunting, and they had a supreme disregard for the havoc done to the crops of the peasantry by game. The Crown systematically broke their power in order to strengthen its own, and it replaced them by its intendants, who were the forerunners of the préfets. Thus the peasant labourers and peasant proprietors came to regard the lords of the soil as the worst kind of drones. Long before the Revolution they had completely lost that feeling of personal loyalty with which they had followed their chiefs to Agincourt and Cressy; and in truth it had been replaced by a passionate hatred of inequality. "Why," was the instinctive idea of the peasant, "should I pay dues, or lift my hat, or feel any reverence for a man who lives upon the sweat of my brow?" That question was certainly not an exhaustive summary of proprietorial rights, but misery is a bad philosopher.

The rebellious instincts of the peasant were strengthened by the writings of Rousseau, who stated the floating principles of a destructive philosophy in a logical shape which was very fascinating to the French, and clothed them with consummate literary form. Thus they speedily helped to make one of the profoundest changes recorded in the history of literature. Nine readers out of ten could easily understand the doctrine that men were naturally equal, that all society was founded on a contract, and that aristocracy was a usurpation unless the common people chose to part with their natural rights. The soil was ready to receive such ideas, and they speedily sprouted up into very grim practical form. Before all the other things, indeed, the Revolution enforced the demand for equality. That claim is serenely treated in England. It is sometimes said to be based on envy ; and such a passion is no doubt powerful in all democratic struggles. But it would be more correct to say that it sprang, in the first place, from the recklessness with which the old French nobles abused their power. They were the most irritating set of tyrants that the caprices of destiny ever set over a quick-witted people. The very keenness of the national intelligence, its ready sympathy, its passion for social intercourse, made the tyranny of the feudal classes more dangerous in France than in any other country. The people were more quick to ask questions, and they more speedily reached a high idea of human dignity. Indeed the sense of human dignity is the tap-root of the spirit of equality.

That sense of human dignity may equally be seen in the national politeness. French peasants and artisans address each other in the same phrases of courtesy as they apply to men of wealth and education, because they have a high idea of self-respect. They are quite at their ease in the presence of the greatest noble, because they have cast off the inherited feelings of serfdom. They are naturally polite because they instinctively give the respect which they exact; and their sense of equality is seen in the courtesy which they offer as well as that which they demand. The same feeling, far more than any mere lurking envy, makes them revolt against the idea that any class may be their rulers by right of birth. And surely there is something worthy of respect in their refusal to let another make laws for them simply because he can trace his ancestry farther back than they, or because he is richer, or because he lives among greater people. After all, it is nothing more than a demand that the man who seeks to rule should produce credentials of his fitness. At all events, the sense of equality is the deepest feeling of the French people. It is the rock on which all their legislators must build. Although Napoleon tried to fritter it away by the creation of new nobles, and although the restored Bourbons attempted to bring back as much as they dared of the old edifice, the passion for equality always reasserts itself.

So far the work of the Revolution was done for ever. Occasionally we may still find in the windows of Legitimist and Catholic booksellers a pamphlet proposing to re-establish the *droit d'aînesse*; but the French pay as little heed to such a demand as we should give to the prayer of a Ritualistic high-churchman that Convocation should get back such legislative power as it possessed in the time of the Tudors. The French Revolution, M. Prévost Paradol said, has failed to found a government, but it has founded a society. The second part of the proposition at least is true. All Frenchmen, except an insignificant minority, agree that, whatever parts of the revolutionary work may be touched, the laws of inheritance shall and must be sacred. No part of their political creed is more puzzling to an average Englishman, and it cannot be understood without such a glance as I have given into the distant recesses of their history.

The French people steadily drifted to universal suffrage; the Royalists learned this with the emphasis of ruin after two generations of effort to support a throne by means of a limited franchise. The artisan fiercely resented his exclusion from political power, not merely because he was prevented from gaining some definite ends, but because the voters were an aristocracy; and the same passion would have disturbed the peasantry so soon as they had learned to take an interest in anything beyond their own fields. Thus the *pays légal,* or the small number of persons who held the electoral power during the reign of Louis Philippe, could only be a halting-place in a democratic country. It is quite possible that too sudden a leap was made in 1848, when the Provisional Government of the Republic established universal suffrage. It was a tremendous experiment to cast the supreme authority into the hands of an ignorant peasantry at one stroke. And the first consequences of the act were disastrous; for it was the strength of rural votes that armed Louis Napoleon with power to overthrow the Republic. Still universal suffrage was inevitable, and on the whole the result of it has been good.

English readers would go very far astray if they were to draw inferences on that subject from the experience of their own country. They may think it reasonable, and even necessary, that the suffrage should be given only to persons who have lived for a certain time in a particular place, who are the heads of households, who pay a certain amount of taxes, or who possess some other "stake in the country." Household suffrage, it may be said, would be better than universal suffrage. No doubt it would be in many countries. But the question whether it would serve as well in France cannot be decided by an appeal to

English customs. An immense difference between the two nations is made, in the first place, by the fact that France has four millions of peasant proprietors. Unlike our own agricultural labourers, they are not mere hired men, with no land or houses of their own, with no savings, with no future, and with a tendency to look for a haven of rest to the workhouse. Industry is their master passion, and they have almost succeeded in converting frugality into a vice. However ignorant such a peasantry may be, they are models of Conservatism, and they form the broad basis on which the political fabric of France must rest. The ownership of the soil must be the main steadying power of a nation, the anchor by which it must ride through the gales that meet every State; but the ownership of a hundred thousand great proprietors is not quite the same thing as that of several millions of peasants. Those of France form the Conservative back-bone of universal suffrage. In her case, therefore, the institution is steadied by an amount of social ballast which would not exist in England. It is quite true, no doubt, that the most solid part of the peasantry would retain their votes even if a high qualification of age and residence should be exacted for the exercise of the franchise, and that the stroke of disfranchisement would fall most heavily on the labourers of the towns, who go from one arrondissement to another in search of work. Such is the very reason which causes the Royalist to be in favour of disfranchisement. The workmen of the towns have shown in the street fights of half-a-dozen revolutions how ready they are to die for a republic. So long as they have votes, the Republican party will always be victorious in the great cities. But the very cause which makes the Royalists eager to sweep away millions of electors renders the Republican party equally determined to resist such a disfranchisement. So far, the contest is a fight for the supremacy of the parties. But much may be said for the individual capacity of the artisans to form sound political opinions. They know the history of

France far better than our own working men know that of England. They take a deeper interest than ours do in public affairs. A glance at the favourite newspapers of the two classes will show how much more highly taught, how much more alive, is the Frenchman. The *Rappel* is usually political from end to end, reports of police cases being pushed into a corner. The corresponding newspapers of England fill their space with records of criminal causes and horse races. The betting ring and the police court are at present the great teachers of the English lower class. But the chief and conclusive argument against any limitation of the suffrage in France is, that such a step would shock the national sentiment of equality. Nothing did so much to weaken the Republic of 1848 as the decree of the Royalist majority that some millions of men should lose their votes. Nothing did so much to strengthen the hands of Prince Louis Bonaparte as that decree, because, although it was proposed by his own ministers and with his own consent, he shrewdly denounced it the instant he saw the signs of popular disgust. In the proclamation announcing the dissolution of the National Assembly, he skilfully made that fact one of the chief indictments against the deputies, and he declared that he himself would restore universal suffrage. For a moment, as Victor Hugo confesses in his "Histoire d'un Crime," the Parisian workmen were misled by the skilful mendacity of that plea, and they would not rise to defend the deputies or the law.

Let universal suffrage be good or bad, it is a necessity in France. And to do it justice we must admit, that it has not yet produced those degrading political effects which are assumed to be inseparable from democracy. Whether it is that the French peasantry are guided by a keen sense of interest, or that the quickness of the national intellect renders it able to see the good of mental power, or that the intense fascination of political combat draws a disproportionately large number of able men to the National Assembly, it is certain that the French Chamber of Deputies need fear no comparison with our own House of Commons in all the qualities which make great legislative bodies.

CHAPTER III.

THE POLITICAL TENDENCIES OF THE CATHOLIC CHURCH.

THE full effect of universal suffrage cannot be seen unless we look from political to religious life. It is little better than a truism to say that there is a close connection between the religion and the politics of a people. Both spring from the same stock of circumstances, tendencies, and traditions. Let us see the one and we can guess the other. That truth may be observed with special vividness in France. The political passions of the country have been twisted into a particular channel by its religious wars and the fate of its Protestantism. At one time the

French people bade fair to be the most Protestant of peoples, and no more beautiful or inspiring chapters have been added to the history of the Church than the pathetic and heroic annals of the Huguenots. Had the Huguenots not been slaughtered on the night of St. Bartholomew, had the Edict of Nantes been replaced by a decree of complete toleration, or even perhaps had that edict not been revoked, Protestantism would have left a religious outlet for the aggressive forces which, from the Renaissance to our own day, have been at war with the traditional authorities of mankind. Such an outlet was given in England by the loose theology of the English Church and the political temper of Puritanism. Hence the Deists of our own land never made many converts beyond a small philosophical coterie. They never made such a change in the popular faith as to provide the requisite number of applauding readers for a Voltaire, and thus no violent break took place in the religion of the country. But from causes which it would take too long to trace, the Huguenots were crushed, and the destruction of French Protestantism left no religious safety-valve for the criticism of the most intellectually aggressive of peoples. Practically, Catholicism in its worst form became for them the only form of Christianity. Men like Voltaire had either to submit their opinions of Newton's philosophy, their views of history, their conceptions of morality to a church which had profited by the iniquities of the Inquisition, and which was responsible for the spirit that had broken Calas on the wheel, or they had to cast themselves loose from religion altogether. What their choice would be could admit of no doubt. Pride of intellect, a sense of human dignity, a hatred of cruelty, a contempt for what would now be roughly called the humbug displayed by pampered and licentious prelates in claiming the authorities of the apostles—all these sentiments made the literary men break out into open war against the Church. The conflict was inevitable, and the store of Christian graces on the side of the Voltaireans was at least as apostolic as the array of those qualities on the side of the Church. But the conflict was none the less disastrous; coming at such a time, it put the vast sources of Catholicism and even the sanctities of religion at the service of political and intellectual bondage, and it tended to fill Liberals with the spirit of irreverence.

The political importance of Catholicism has been greatly increased in France by the change which has come over the temper and the discipline of the whole Papal Church. Few things, in the history of that community, are more remarkable than the growing tendency to centralise its power in Rome. At one time each national Church had peculiarities of ritual and a great measure of independence. The Gallican Church, in particular, made good its claim to have a large degree of freedom in theological as well as in practical affairs. The charter of that Church was for a century those famous articles which declared the Pope to be infallible only when he spoke as the organ of an Œcumenical Council; and the clergy never forgot that their Church was French as well as Catholic. It is true that the chief author of the Gallican articles and the most illustrious defender of Gallican liberties, Bossuet himself, practically admitted that Rome was the court of last appeal, in the dispute between himself and Fénelon respecting the theology of the Quietists. In all such moments of trial, the most intrepid champions of Gallican freedom found themselves forced, in practice if not in theory, to confess the infallibility of Rome. It is true that the absolute assertion of the principle was fated to follow the unvarying example. Still the French clergy had once a large amount of independence, and hence a distinctly national character. In some ways Catholicism was a federation of national churches, each possessing such state rights as greatly limited the power of the central government. But Gallicanism is now as much a thing of the past as the regal splendour of Versailles. If there are any Gallicans among the clergy of France they hide in corners, and they can scarcely speak without being called heretics. The Roman Breviary has now taken the place of the Gallican; the Gallican articles would be accounted heresy by the most lax of French theologians; and the Pope is as absolutely the master of the several bishops as the bishops are the masters of the inferior clergy. No prelate would now dream of resisting even the political dictation of the Vatican; and the dependence of the priests is described with as much truth as vividness by the famous boast of Cardinal de Bonnechose, Archbishop of Rouen. "*Mon clergé*," he said, "*sont un régiment, et quand je lui dit, 'Marchez,' il marche.*" The first Napoleon imagined that he could prevent the clergy from being dependent upon Rome by means of the Concordat, which virtually enables the civil power to fill up every diocese by presenting to the Pope the ecclesiastic whom it wishes him to instal, and by making the clergy look to the State for their stipends. But, in one all-important respect, that compact is fatally different from the old Gallican guarantees. Before the Revolution, the clergy owned a large part of the soil, and hence they were a feudal aristocracy as well as a sacerdotal caste. Nothing did so much to make them remember that they were Frenchmen as their immense stake in the material interests of their country. But no such memory is aroused by the pinched salaries which are annually doled out to them by the State, which they believe to be a beggarly restitution for the robbery of their lands, and which, as they are constantly warned by the Radicals, and as they learn from the signs of the times, may be stopped by a vote of the Chamber. The Concordat would have failed, however, even if it had re-endowed the Church with her ancient property. It has failed because no artificial compacts can resist the force of general tendencies; and for centuries the general tendency of Catholicism has been to concentrate power in the hands of Rome. In that respect the Catholic Church repeats with extraordinary and instinctive closeness the later history of the empire of which she was the heir. As Rome grew in size, she had to lodge more and more power with some one man, in order that he might curb the anarchical tendencies of the capital and keep in check the distant provinces. That necessity became overmastering when the Barbarians began to assert their power on the frontiers, to wrest back the conquests of the empire, and even to threaten the old home of the republic. The central power had to be strengthened, until the whole Roman world was the slave even of a Nero or a Domitian. Nor could the process of centralisation cease until the fabric of imperialism toppled and fell to ruin. Whatever Burke may say, the medicine of the constitution must sometimes be made its daily food, even at the cost of ultimate decay.

The laws of human nature do not change

merely because men invent steam-engines and read daily newspapers. The necessities of imperial power and their attendant maladies will live as long as human passions and interests. The necessities of imperial Rome are repeated in the daily life of its theocratic successor; in the Papacy as in the Empire, the first condition of rule is unity. But there is an immense tendency towards disintegration in a dominion stretching to the end of the earth, and including a hundred nations, and tongues, and races, and histories, and masses of inherited traditions. Every national church is liable to drift towards independence. Every great leader of every national church is prompted to be a reformer, and is therefore liable to be a heresiarch. Since the Reformation, and in particular since the French Revolution, the perils of disunion have been multiplied by a process which repeats in a spiritual form the irruption of the Barbarians. The many and vigorous sects of Protestantism, the motley bands of Rationalism, the aggressive

POLITICAL TENDENCIES OF CATHOLIC CHURCH. 43

Voltaireans, the dreamy disciples of Rousseau, the evangelists of the ideas sown by the French Revolution, all the young, unorganised, hungry, bold spirits in the empire of intellect and belief, are to the Papacy what the Goths and the Vandals were to decaying Rome. They have wrested from it some of its vast dominions. They are settling in its oldest provinces. They are defeating its trained legions; and they believe that they are the heirs of the great theocracy. The only way to keep the spiritual empire together is to tighten the bonds of discipline even at the cost of stifling all provincial independence, and to give the Papacy a power at once clear and absolute of stopping all disputes. As the centrifugal forces of the Church constantly tend to make the outlying planets of the Papal system fly into heretical space, proportionably greater must be made the centripetal power of Rome. That necessity has the strength of an instinct rather than a theory, and the Pope would have grown into a Cæsar even if he had sought to guard provincial liberties.

Such was the root of De Maistre's argument that, in a divinely ordered church, the Pope must be infallible, because all sovereigns must act as if they could not err, and because the infallibility of a single ecclesiastical ruler is more convenient than that of the six or seven hundred prelates who form the cumbersome divinity of an Œcumenical Council. Such was also the origin of the Vatican Council and the Decree of Infallibility. Such is the reason why all the Roman Catholic clergy are now Ultramontane in temper. Ultramontanism can be explained without the aid of Jesuit conspiracies, for it simply expresses the collective instincts of self-interest in the greatest organisation which the world has seen since the fall of imperial Rome.

The change, however, is none the less important for France, because it has weakened and almost destroyed the secular ties which bound the clergy to the nation. They have ceased to understand what patriotism means when it comes into conflict with loyalty to Rome. In vain does the Govern-

POLITICAL TENDENCIES OF CATHOLIC CHURCH. 45

ment nominate the bishops; it must nominate Ultramontanes now that the Gallicans are extinct. In vain are they reminded of their duty to the State. What is their duty to an infidel Government in comparison with their duty to the Vicar of Christ? Their country is the Church, and they will not again be Frenchmen until France shall be ruled, as she was in the days of her old kings, by the light of Catholicism.

The political importance of the change in the spirit of the Roman Church has been further increased by one of the most interesting movements of our time. This has been an age, not only of scientific inquiry but of religious revival, and the spiritual emotion has been spread at least as widely as the reverence for inductive truth. Just as maladies mysteriously pass from land to land, the seeds of them appearing to float in the air and to be borne by unseen currents; just as new ideas, the seeds of a Renaissance or a French revolution, burst out at nearly the same time in widely separated centres of thought, so has this age seen the great old religions of Asia and Europe quickened by the pulse of a new life. India and the Turkish Empire, America and England, have all been powerfully moved by the wave of passion; and on France it has left as deep traces as in any other land. Just as the rise of the Jesuits followed the first triumphs of Protestantism, and just as the Church of Rome wrenched back by one evangel much of what she had lost by another, so has French Catholicism drawn new vigour, power of expression, and depth of piety from the triumphant irreverence of the French Revolution. A fresh political as well as religious force was thrown into her public life by the outburst of fervour which will for ever be connected with the names of Lamennais, Montalembert, and Lacordaire. Better than any abstract dissertation does the life of Lamennais show the longing felt by great masses of the French people for a worthy spiritual belief, the fervour which a new faith has brought to some, and the hopeless disappointment with which it has embittered others. When Lamennais's mind was filled with all the political ideas of democracy; his temper was despotic, and so were his methods. In the early part of his career it was the absolutism of the Church which he strove to establish; but she was to enforce the principles of modern Liberalism. In his later days, after he had failed to convert the Pope to the political faith of the French Revolution, and after he had drifted far away from Rome, he equally sought to set up the despotism of democracy and the Republic. Such compromises between religion and the world as Gallicanism or the Concordat were not more hateful to the theological austerity of his younger days, when Pope Leo XII. called him "the last of the Fathers," than the constitutionalism of Louis Philippe was to the Republican fervour of his later faith, when the people had taken the place of the Church in his heated and gloomy imagination, when he thought kings the chief scourges of mankind and democracy the evangel sent for the healing of the nations. Lamennais may take rank with Joseph de Maistre as the great preacher of Ultramontanism in its modern and its extreme form. An extraordinary force was given to his teaching, not less by its aptness for a time in which masses of men were sick of political and religious compromise, than by the strength of his individuality, and by an eloquence, destitute indeed of French lightness and pliancy and sunny ease, but Hebrew in the richness and the majesty of its imagery, and steeped in the gloom of Breton woods and melodious with the wail of Breton seas. Altogether he is the most impressive figure amongst recent Frenchmen. Around him gathered, in Lacordaire and Gerbet and Montalembert, ardent, young, aggressive souls. Like him, they were disgusted by Voltaireanism and all forms of impiety. Like him, they were sick of the hallelujahs sung over the triumphs of material progress. They would not admit that the best part of man had been made a whit better by big factories or steam-engines, and they went back for their ideals to the despised ages of faith, and for their exemplars to the saints of the Catholic calendar. At the same time those young soldiers of the Church fancied like Lamennais himself that they could unite the rebellious principles of the Revolution with the doctrines which they had inherited from the remote days of authority. How gallantly they battled to persuade the Church that she should abandon the pay and fling off the restraints of the State; how they strove to make education clerical by making it free; how, above all, they went to Rome to defend their creed before the Pope himself and to enlist him in the Liberal camp—all this forms the most beautiful and not the least noble chapter of religious Quixotism in the history of modern France. Of course they failed. The Church would not give up her pay; the State would not abandon its scholastic hold on the young; and ecclesiastics would not rub shoulders with Mirabeau and Danton. Hence Lamennais drifted away to more congenial work, leaving Montalembert and Lacordaire to fight, with their right hands tied, for what they deemed the twin cause of Catholicism and Liberty.

Of course they failed again; the life of both was embittered by the discovery that the official teachers of Catholicism were implacably hostile to all kinds of Liberalism. Lacordaire was silenced; Montalembert fell away for a time from the Liberal camp, and took service under the grimy banner of Louis Napoleon. Repenting of that unworthy alliance with the hero of the pact between the sacristy and the barrack-room, he nevertheless remained in his strange position. The evening of his too short and not unchivalrous life was darkened by the proclamation, in the Syllabus and the dogma of infallibility, of decrees which, he feared, would cut off the Church from all contact with modern liberty. No doubt his apprehensions ought to have presaged those codifications of old claims; but the awakening from his dreamland was none the less rude. Both he and Lacordaire had attempted an impossible task. Nevertheless, they and Lamennais had helped to produce a vast effect on the private and public life of their country. Before their active years, church-going had no doubt been made fashionable by the courts of Louis XVIII. and Charles X. It had been made so fashionable, that rough blaspheming generals, who had learned their manners under the Empire, found it necessary to become regular attendants at mass, and to learn the superficial ways of good Catholics. Montalembert was the sign rather than the cause of the great reaction. But he did powerfully help to enlist the enthusiasm of the young on the side of Catholicism. The fervour of the French nobles for the Pope, the readiness of their sons to serve in the ranks of the Papal Zouaves, and their pilgrimages to Lourdes, cannot be thoroughly understood without a survey of the religious movement which was partly symbolised, and partly led by Lamennais and Montalembert.

CHAPTER IV.

THE CLERICAL PARTY.

FROM that movement we may date the rise of a party which deserves to be closely studied; a party which has its members among the Legitimists, the Orleanists, and the Bonapartists, and which will soon have them among even perhaps the Republicans; a party which is much less careful about its weapons than about its ends—and that is the Clerical party. Its purpose is to strengthen the power of the Catholic Church. Many of its members are guided, of course, by a spirit of pure religious devotion, or by a fanaticism which, if unreasonable, is free from any taint of political ambition. Such men trace most of the evils which have befallen France to the impiety which was the herald and the follower, the cause and the effect, of the Revolution. Voltaire, they think, sneered away the reverence of the people for king, country, family honour, all the sanctities which ennoble life. He was a grinning devil, and De Maistre, the ablest of the Clerical teachers, said that everyone who liked him was a bad man. Hence the recent outburst of Catholic wrath against the celebration of the hundredth anniversary of his death. Diderot and the band of the Encyclopædists finished the work which the master spirit had begun. Thus, losing the tie of morality and religion, the French, we are told, became a herd of struggling, warring units, who pulled down throne, aristocracy, and Church in sheer wantonness. Nor has France—add the Clerical party—yet reaped the full harvest of the seed sown by Voltaire and his fellow-labourers. She is still irreverent and irreligious. There are grave blots on her family life. She has no ideals higher than military glory or secular republics.

Honeycombed by practical atheism, she has nothing to purify her private or public life, nor anything to bind her together as she was clasped by the dogmas and the hierarchies of the mediæval Church. Hence her factions fight with each other for selfish supremacy, political warfare is a game of vile passions, and the great France of other days drifts from one revolution to another. Secular teaching is the nurse of atheism, which is the parent of republicanism, which in turn generates anarchy. There is only one way to purify and exalt and strengthen the nation, and that is to restore its old religious faith. Therefore, the Catholic Church must take her ancient place at the head of society, and above all she must be entrusted with the duty of teaching the young.

Such is the doctrine of those political Catholics, who sincerely believe in the doctrines of their own Church. But all the members of the Clerical party are not religious enthusiasts. On the contrary, unless their good name is made the sport of calumny, a great many of them have as little real belief in the dogmas of the Church as the open followers of Voltaire. Victor Hugo, in his "Quatre-Vingt Treize," describes such a character in a Breton noble, the Marquis de Lantenac. A fanatical champion of the Church as well as of the monarchy, he regards the enemy of both as vermin, to be stamped out rather than argued with or converted. But he puts aside, with a grand and slightly satirical bow, the vulgar question, whether the Church is rightly informed about everything which she teaches. A gentleman might have thoughts of his own on that subject, but he must keep them to himself. To recite his sceptical musings in the hearing of the mob would be to cast reproach on the throne and the nobility, because the Church had taken those institutions into her keeping, and was their chief guardian. Christianity was revealed, in fact, to provide the French nobles with private chaplains, and to keep the multitude in awe of their betters. Such characters as Lantenac, reduced from the Michael Angelo-like proportions of Victor Hugo to the petty scale of ordinary life, may still be found among the Legitimists. Frenchmen would smile at the idea that some noted members of the Clerical party really believed the Pope to be infallible, or to be anything else than the spiritual head of an international Scotland Yard. Their feelings are partially expressed with brilliant cynicism by Heine, who was as little of a believer as Voltaire himself, although his Hebrew blood gave him a profoundly deeper sense of spiritual things. He was an atheist, he said, so long as atheistical theories were confined to philosophic supper-parties; but when they passed to the smoky meetings of vulgar artisans, and when grimy mechanics chattered materialistic doctrines, he was converted by his sense of refinement, and he awoke out of his irreligious dream. He saw that dogmatic religion, whether true or not, helped to keep down the surges of pinched ferocity. Heine's example has been largely followed in France. Her official religious ceremonies are demurely attended by men who, if we may trust the voice of satire, do not know how to use the holy water brush. But it may be admitted that such ignorance is very exceptional. Even the incredulous members of the Clerical party have perfectly learned the drill of their faith.

The Clerical faction, such as we know it, was not organised until the Republic of 1848 had been established. Down to that time, the little group of parliamentary statesmen who "managed" the *pays légal* of two hundred thousand voters had not lost the old jealousy of priestly influence. The Revolution of 1830 had been made by the middle class, which had been profoundly moved by the spirit of Voltaire. The leaders of the movement which overthrew the throne of Charles X. were all eager to keep the clergy away from the polling-booths and from the National Assembly. Louis Philippe himself was in religious creed a good-humoured tolerant cynic of the eighteenth century. The note of the movement is sounded in Béranger's songs, which express with incomparable power the lightness, the gaiety, and the hard common-sense of his countrymen. He is never more effective than when he satirises the pretensions of the priests. The bishops instinctively felt that the new monarchy was less favourable to the Church than the old, and for a moment some of them were disposed to treat Louis Philippe as a usurper. But the rebellious prelates were soon brought to reason by the Minister of Public Worship, the Duc de Broglie, the father of the statesman who lately led the Clerical party with a skill untempered by scruple. The Government, the House of Peers, and the Chamber of Deputies also showed how determined they were to uphold the secular spirit of the State by their refusal to let Montalembert and Lacordaire open an infant school without the warrant of the university.

But a vast change in that temper was made by the Revolution of 1848. Hitherto the rebellious instincts of the artisans had been kept pretty well in hand. Although they had shed their blood during the days of July, they had not been rewarded with power. Their dream of a republic had been rudely broken by the intimation that Louis Philippe was "*le meilleur des républiques*," and all their attempts to shake his power had been defeated with an iron hand. But meanwhile they had been greedily listening to the Socialistic teachings of the St. Simonians and of Louis Blanc. They had been taught to believe that the work of 1789 would be incomplete so long as the old forms of society were left unchanged. They had been encouraged to think that the State could abolish pauperism and even poverty. Louis Napoleon himself had given some encouragement to that idea in one of the dreamy pamphlets which he composed during his imprisonment at Ham. When the constitutional monarchy was thrown down, the Socialistic mob of Paris seemed to threaten the very existence of society. In M. Louis Blanc it had an eloquent and devoted representative in the Provisional

Government itself. Thus the rich feared that the Socialistic teaching would make the poor rise against the rich, that there would be a systematic attack on property, and that France would be shaken by the worst of all convulsions —a war of classes.

That fear was deepened by the first great act of the Provisional Government, which was the establishment of universal suffrage. Thus had the waves of democracy swept away that little *pays légal* which was the masterpiece of Louis Philippe's government. Thus had the supreme power been transferred at one stroke from two hundred thousand voters to eight millions. Ledru Rollin, who was the chief author of that change, effected perhaps as great a revolution by a stroke of his pen as the Convention did when it beheaded the king. Henceforward all the towns would be ruled, not by a group of essentially Conservative, if somewhat Voltairean, shopkeepers, but by an unknown throng of artisans, steeped in the violent traditions of the first Republic, and deluded by the Socialistic fancies of more dangerous, if less gifted, leaders than Rousseau.

But Ledru Rollin's act has created a still more important political class in the peasantry. Universal suffrage may almost be said to have called into political being that great and hitherto inert mass which is the foundation of French society. In the peasantry, as I have already said, we find that marvellous industry which is as characteristic of the French people as their gaiety; that thrift which has been the wonder of Europe ever since the war with Germany; that Conservatism which has anchored France to the social institutions of 1789 in spite of all her changes of dynasty. But there also may be found in equal measure an ignorance which casts its shadow over the most highly polished and cultivated of nations. That ignorance, however, had been good for the Catholic Church, since it had kept them free from the aggressive scepticism of the great towns. Voltaire and Diderot and Rousseau were almost as little known in the Dordogne as in the wilds of Inverness-shire. The peasants still went to mass on Sundays and saints'-days; their wives and daughters went to confession; and the whole class was Catholic in a quiet way. Here therefore seemed a vast unorganised throng, which would follow the Clerical party in political things, which would outweigh the democratic scepticism and radicalism of the great towns, and which might give the Conservative managers more than an equivalent for the loss of the *pays légal*. Here then was a common ground of action for such statesmen as M. Thiers and M. de Montalembert, although the Orleanist chief was notoriously a Voltairean rather than a Catholic in theology. Like the Catholic leader, he was afraid of the many-headed monster of democracy which the Republic had unchained. Terrified by the philosophic attacks on the institution of property and by the Socialistic temper of the artisans, he no longer dared to despise the political power with which the Clerical party offered to arm the enemies of the Republic, if they would help it to reach some of its political ends. M. Thiers was a very different man in 1848 from what he became on the morrow of a mighty national calamity, when as President of the Republic he found that freedom might give a nation more stability than an alliance between the priests and the police. From a union of the old parliamentary chiefs with the leaders of the political Catholics came two memorable events—the expedition to Rome and a change in the system of national education. But for M. Thiers and his party, the forces of the French Republic would not have been used to crush the Republic of Rome. In his interesting conversation with Mr. Nassau Senior, he said that he favoured the sending of the French troops to prevent Austria from gaining a hold over Rome. The purpose of that expedition, he declared, was to defend French interests. "It was for the sake of France he maintained; it was to plant the French flag in the castle of St. Angelo; it was to maintain our right to have one half of Italy if Austria seized the other. Rather than see the Austrian eagle on the flagstaff that rises above the Tiber, I would destroy a hundred constitutions and a hundred religions." But M. Thiers and the other Orleanist chiefs had a much more powerful reason for proposing to fit out the expedition to Rome. He and they wished to put down the secular republic which, by pushing aside the temporal power of the Pope, had trampled on the chief symbol of vested interests and the monarchy. That republic unpleasantly recalled the Convention of 1793. Mazzini and Garibaldi bore an uncomfortable likeness to the better chiefs of that grim body, and their republic would have been an aggressive reality. It would have speedily destroyed all the smaller states of Italy, fired the Republican party of France with the energy of a great example of weakened authority in every part of Europe. Secular and sceptical minds like M. Thiers could so far join with Catholic minds like M. de Montalembert, as to admit that if the Roman revolutionists should succeed, a fatal blow would be struck at the system of treaties which he thought determined the boundaries of modern states and helped to keep kings on their thrones. M. Thiers knew that several of the European states were in great degree built artificially. At the same time he was the very type of the man who fearlessly sits down at a council table to decide with map and pencil how people shall be grouped and whom they shall obey. The principle that they should be grouped according to their nationalities, and be asked to say under what government they should like to live, was a principle which, in the opinion of M. Thiers, would lead straight to anarchy. Thus all the Whigs of France—and he was the chief of the sect—believed that with the establishment of the Roman republic would begin the destruction of monarchical arrangement for the bridling of democracy. The members of the Clerical party were led by simpler motives. To them the blow aimed at the temporal power of the Pope seemed struck at religion itself, and it would be followed, they thought, by attacks on the temporal possessions of the Catholic Church throughout the world. Thus the expedition to Rome was a bond of union between the secular Conservatives and the Catholics. A Republican would not scruple to add that it was the sacrament of their joint infamy. At least it had a profoundly disastrous effect on the future fortunes of France, both abroad and at home.

The Clerical party won a still greater triumph by attacking the system of public instruction, which bears the marks of Napoleon's genius for despotism. The Revolution swept away the old provincial colleges, and when Napoleon reached the Consulate the time had not yet come for applying the gratuitous and obligatory system which had been among the good dreams of the Convention. So he founded a series of lycées, or great public schools, and endowed them with a multitude of scholarships. He established, or he shaped, the colleges for technical instruction; finally, when he became emperor, he grouped all these institutions under a central university, which alone could give certificates of competence to teach, or to practise any of the higher professions. His half-military lycées, as M. Renan has pointed out, were founded on the model of the Jesuit colleges; and, in truth, the genius of the Jesuits was closely akin to his own. His hope was that the children of all classes and political parties should be found on the same benches; that all should be taught by professors devoted to the Revolution and to him; that the spirit of his rule should thus reach the homes of the Bourbonists, the devotees of the Church, and the puritans of the Republic; and that thus the discords of France should at last be healed. The influence of the Revolution, and its Napoleonic corrective, would also, he thought, be felt in the humblest of village schools, because the central university—which would only be the State under another name—should dictate what each child should learn. Such was, perhaps, the most gigantic and searching of intellectual despotisms ever fashioned outside the Church of Rome. In effect it has been a mighty secular propaganda, because it has been set in motion by essentially secular statesmen. If it has not served the purpose of the Empire, it has, at least, helped to deepen the lessons of the Revolution. But the Catholic Church could not be expected to tolerate rivalry in her own field with weapons borrowed from herself, and she has made ceaseless war against the autocratic university. Lacordaire and Montalembert were punished for attempting, in 1831, to open an infant school without the license of the State; but the celebrated prosecution of these young zealots led the way to a breach in the Napoleonic system. During the reign of Louis Philippe the clergy saw more and more clearly that they had everything to learn from freedom of teaching. The prowess of their order in Belgium showed them how they might thus use the revolutionary weapon of liberty for the ends of a despotic Church. Many secular minds, for the reasons which I have already stated, were won over to their side. M. de Falloux, the political chief of the Clerical party, when Louis Napoleon made him Minister of Public Instruction in 1849, was able to form a commission which made a serious inroad in the old monopoly. It did so by giving the higher clergy seats in the Council of Public Instruction and in the academical councils of the provinces. It did so, above all, by providing that certificates of competence from the university should no longer be exacted from all teachers. These changes, which were sanctioned by an essentially Royalist assembly, enabled the Roman Catholic clergy to gain a powerful hold over the springs of popular teaching. The Brothers of the Congregation—a half-priestly body, wearing almost the same garb, and taking nearly the same vows as the clergy—are now spread over the whole of France. They teach in the elementary schools. As they are unmarried, and do not follow their calling for the sake of profit, they cost the communes less than secular teachers. The Jesuits, who busy themselves with the higher education, have planted colleges in several parts of France;

and they almost exclusively instruct the sons of the richer Royalist families. In one of their Parisian houses they also prepare, with much success, young men for the Polytechnic and the military colleges. In 1875 the Clericals made a determined effort to destroy the remains of the academical monopoly by demanding power to institute independent universities, which should have the right, not merely to teach, but to grant degrees. They were successful. One section of the Republican party is enraged at what it holds to be a crusade, not for education but for the Church; and for the Church, not as a spiritual but as a political body.

A sketch of the Clerical party would be incomplete without some account of two remarkable men who, each in his own way, have been its guides. I mean M. Dupanloup and M. Louis Veuillot. The Bishop of Orleans was at one time supposed to be a Gallican, and he did show signs of independence at the Council of the Vatican, by stoutly contending that to proclaim the infallibility of the Pope would be inopportune. He sometimes even betrayed a spirit of independence and even waywardness, which made the Frenchman gleam through the Catholic. But no one was more persuaded than he that all the calamities of France dated from the rejection of the Catholic faith, and he carried on an unpitying war against every form of infidelity. He left the French Academy because it elected, in M. Littré, a man who has no belief in any higher teaching than that of science, and who thinks that evolution explains the myriad varieties of organic life and the discordant crowd of religions and moralities. At the same time Monseigneur Dupanloup was a man of literary culture, and he was not afraid to contend, against the bigotry of his order, that the Roman and the Grecian classics must have a place in any scheme of Christian education. He was supposed to be the Bossuet of these latter days—the only kind of Bossuet which the new Gallican Church is able to fashion. His style is not quite such a model of all the higher rhetorical qualities as that of the man who wrote the "Oraisons Funèbres;" but it is vigorous, terribly ready, and as free from ambiguity as the scolding of the street. If not quite a Bossuet, he was a superior "Henry of Exeter." A trenchant pamphleteer of the old school — an incarnate denial of the precept, "Blessed are the meek" — the bishop was ever warring against some form of practical scepticism, and the centenaire festival in honour of Voltaire drew from him a characteristic explosion of wrath against the supreme literary enemy of his Church. But he was much more than a master of fluent vituperation. He was a man of some political sagacity, and he had so much force of character that he might have had a considerable career as a statesman a hundred and fifty years ago. His native shrewdness freed him from a bigoted liking for any one form of government, and he would have supported the Republic if it would have given itself into the hands of the Church. But, as a Liberal

Republic must be anti-Catholic, Monseigneur Dupanloup pursued the government with passionate hostility. It had no more relentless foe; and, as he was certain that it was doing the work of the devil, he was able to attack it without the hindrance of scruple. Such was his influence over the women who were highly placed in political society, and over the men whom they guided, that he wielded a great deal of unseen power; and it is supposed that he did as much as any person to bring about the combination which, on the 16th May, 1877, attempted to overturn the Republic. What he wanted was a government which, whether imperial or monarchical, Legitimist or parliamentary, should be Clerical; a government which should give the education of the young into the hands of the priesthood, and virtually make the Jesuits the academical instructors of France; which should befriend the Pope and watch for a chance of restoring his temporal power; and which, in one word, would make constant unpitying war against the accursed principles of the Revolution.

The editor of the *Univers* has much less influence amongst political men than had the Bishop of Orleans, but he more faithfully reflects the true spirit of his Church. Although a secular writer, he is more theological than the prelate, and indeed he has no other canon of belief than the will of the Pope. No political difficulties come in his way, for political difficulties are infinitely contemptible in the eyes of a man to whom the Church is all in all. What does it matter if so wretched a thing as a republic or a parliamentary monarchy should perish in striving to wrest the heritage of the Papacy from robber hands? A Legitimist monarchy is more respectable than the Republic, because, like the Church herself, it is built on the spirit of obedience to authority. Thus it smites the impious self-conceit of mankind, and thus its interests would force it to do battle for religion and the Holy Father. But

France will not accept a Legitimist king. She will not so far bend her proud and anti-Christian spirit as to recognise her rightful masters. She has ceased to believe in God. She is given over to the lust of the eye and the pride of life, and hence there will come to her such vengeance as awaits the enemies of Heaven. M. Veuillot's speculations are disturbed by none of the vain subtilties which perplex men who call themselves thinkers or philosophers. He knows such men; he has found them out. They are all charlatans, fools, or knaves. It is the wickedness of their hearts which keeps them away from the fold of the Church, or makes them question her divine right to tell Mr. Darwin that he is a presumptuous fool for pretending to trace the pedigree of good Catholics back to apes.

Had M. Veuillot no other distinction than such ideas, he would be as vulgar a personage as any priest who delivers a Lenten discourse on the atheistic tendencies of science. But he has moral and literary distinctions. He brings into religious discussion the malignity and the invective of which he made himself a master when he was still in the camp of the unconverted, and a writer for the *petite presse* of Paris. As his change of life and creed was very sudden, he had no time, in the middle passage of repentance, to get rid of the bad passions, or to blunt the unscrupulous epigrams, which gave him daily bread when he trifled for the *Figaro*. "So his writings," as I have said elsewhere, "are the most wonderful pieces of rhetoric ever laid at the feet of the Church. They are such as might be written by a haunter of cafés and theatres, a fast man about town, a reader of loose novels, a master of profane swearing, an orator of the democratic clubs, if all these personages were rolled into one tremendous compound, and if the corporate profanity were to be converted in a single night to the faith that all Voltaireans are scoundrels, that the real crown of thorns is kept under lock and seal by the Archbishop of Paris, that crowds of miracles are worked at Lourdes, and that forty-nine people have been raised from the dead at Notre Dame de Lumières of Marseilles. The conversion of a single night would, of course, leave many traces of the last night's merriment, riot, or debauch. . . . The convert would display no change of spirit, but only a change of antipathies. He would curse what he had been wont to bless, and bless what he had been wont to curse; but that would be all. . . . Thus the editor of the *Univers* gives us a Christianity which has been soaked in the mud of the Quartier Latin and the *cafés chantants*, a Christianity which has kept late hours, and has been about town for a few centuries. Its best quality is its virile and frank ferocity, for it gives the new commandment, that if a man strike thee on the one cheek thou shalt hit him back, and hit hard. . . . In his old state he believed nothing in particular, because the Quartier Latin, the cafés and the *petite presse* were armed with no Œcumenical Council. But he is now as definite as if he kept an Œcumenical Council in his inkbottle."*

M. Veuillot is eagerly read by the unconverted throng of Frenchmen because he writes an admirably vigorous, glowing, and epigrammatic style. There is, on the whole, no more effective journalist in Europe; and Frenchmen would not be such literary artists as they are, if they did not like to see themselves damned in the best of French. But he is not so much admired by the more Liberal of the Catholic clergy, and, in truth, he has pursued them with relentless calumny, jeering, and invective, because his shrewd mother wit makes him see that they are blinded by mischievous delusions. He has said that "there is not, and that there cannot be, such a thing as Liberal Catholicism." "A Liberal," he adds, with pungent truth, "is not a Catholic, and a Catholic is not a Liberal." Thus does M. Veuillot strike the real note of his

* *Spectator*, Dec. 6, 1873.

Church. A Liberal Archbishop of Paris, Monseigneur Sibour, was once so enraged at his tone and temper as to prohibit the clergy from reading the *Univers*. But the journalist was defended by other prelates and sheltered by the Vatican. There could be no more eloquent sign of episcopal subjection than the fact that a distinguished prelate, in the greatest diocese in the world, should thus have been ignominiously compelled to withdraw from a contest with an unsanctified layman. Thanks to the protection of the Papacy, and to his own literary talents, M. Veuillot has become a more important power in France than any of the bishops themselves. He gives the law to the country clergy and he dictates to their episcopal superiors. The Vatican makes such use of him as it used to make of the preaching friars, who, directly commissioned by itself, might go into every diocese, might teach without fear of episcopal censure, and if they were hindered by bishop or king, might carry their complaints direct to

Rome. The Church has no longer the old employment for the Franciscans and the Dominicans. The preaching friars of our day are the writers for the Catholic press, and the chief of them is M. Louis Veuillot. He is the St. Dominic of these days, and he has discovered no contemptible substitute for the thumb-screw of the Inquisition in the invectives and the calumnies which he learned to wield when he lived in the literary slums of unbelief, and was an inspired *gamin de Paris*. The editor of the *Univers* is about the last person to whom the devout would go for the charities of the Gospel, and it is a satire on the Church of Bossuet and Fénelon that its most effective pen should be wielded by a man whom nature intended to be a writer for the *Figaro*. Nor would anyone dream of finding in his rich prose a gleam of philosophical understanding. He is the Cobbett of his Church. But his impatience of subtilties makes him a better representative of average Catholicism than men of finer spirit. If we would see what must be the political temper of Catholicism in this age of rationalistic Goths and Vandals, we cannot afford to miss the picturesque and perfectly convinced malignity of M. Louis Veuillot.

Such men as M. Veuillot have their antitheological counterparts in the camp of the Republicans. Indeed, the enemies of the Clerical party are quite as fanatical as the members of that party itself. And, just as the one faction gathers round the most compact, skilful, worldly, and successful of religious orders, so does the other find a symbol of combat in the name of the man who, taught in youth by that order, became the greatest literary enemy of its Church. The influence of that society and of that writer is felt everywhere in France. At the end of every avenue to political power stands Loyola or Voltaire — Loyola disguised and Voltaire disguised, but as characteristic in their vehemence as when in life they battled for supremacy. The more scoffing kind of Voltaireanism, it is true, has gone out of fashion. Men of culture, even when they do honour to Voltaire's marvellous gifts, admit that his critical methods would now be coarse and ineffective. The finer sceptical minds are quick to confess the debt which Europe owes to the mediæval Church. Much of M. Littré's book, "Etudes sur les Barbares et le Moyen Age," might have been written by a devout Catholic, and Montalembert himself has paid no higher tributes to the sanctity of mediæval Catholicism than M. Renan. Even a fervid friend of the Church might scruple to say, with the author of "Etudes d'Histoire Religieuse," that, if he were condemned for life to read but one book, he would choose the Bollandist Lives of the Saints. The cultivated critics of the Church are careful to mark the contrast between the religion which expressed the highest teaching of a past age and the religion which is contradicted by the highest teaching of ours. They oppose Catholicism chiefly because they think that its political and moral influence is hurtful to the best tendencies of our time. In practice they do not fight it the less vigorously because they see what good it did centuries ago. Many of them feel conscientiously bound to leave directions in their wills that they shall be buried with purely civil rites. Such was the command of Lamennais; such was the command of St. Beuve; and such is the order left by all the more fervid members of the Radical party. They would be accounted renegades if they did not thus protest against the spiritual and political claims of the Church with all the solemnity of the grave. And a fiercer spirit is found in the ranks which furnished the Commune with its more ardent spirits. The artisans of the great towns regard the Roman Catholic clergy with a feeling which is softened neither by respect for religion itself, nor by any knowledge of what the Church has done for civilisation. It is a feeling of something like sheer hatred. M. Jules Favre was once asked to subscribe a declaration of atheism, in order to show that he

was worthy to be trusted by the democracy of
Lyons. Such a demand is not uncommon among
the class which furnish the material of volcanic
passions, and it betrays a temper which left
terrible memorials of its fury in the last days
of the Commune. That spirit springs in part
from the tradition, that the priests have ever
taken the side of the rich and the powerful
against the poor and the lowly. It is also caused
by the inevitable interference of the clergy with
private as well as public life. The priest lays
claim to mystic graces infinitely more exalted than
any that Bossuet ever attributed to Louis XIV.
The French bear such pretensions less patiently
than any other people, because they have a
stronger sense than any other of human equality.
And they have seen too many proofs that the
claims of the priesthood are no empty show.
They know that the influence of the Church has
been used to buttress a hated monarchy, and to
overthrow a passionately loved republic. They
believe that it has produced wars which have

brought incalculable woes to France. But the main root of their dislike springs from a profounder soil. It springs from the instinctive feeling that, resting on authority and relying on absolute obedience, the Church must wage a war to the death against the spirit of the Revolution, because that spirit is essentially rationalistic, because it will have no hierarchies save such as depend on free election or personal qualities, and because it will recognise no transmitted claims to exact obedience. Thus the Church has not only taken the side of absolutism, military rule, and privileged classes, but, by nursing the spirit of obedience to inherited authority, she has given the majority of her devotees a powerful bias against the Republic.

The Catholic Church has built one type of society; the spirit of the Revolution is building another; and in France, at least, the two are profoundly and implacably hostile. Ultimately they will not be able to live together unless one or other should greatly change. Either

Catholicism must give up its political pretensions or the Democratic Republicans must abandon their ideals.

Liberal Catholics, it is true, hope for a day of reconciliation between the two camps. In the doctrines and the constitution of the Church there is nothing, they say, hostile to a democratic society or a republican government. She finds herself at home in America; why should she not find herself at home in France, when the memory of old strifes shall have become dim? Books have been written to show that the "principles of '89," if properly understood, might be taught from the pulpit. The political difficulties of the Syllabus itself have been explained away by intrepid casuists. Father Curci, one of the ablest as well as the boldest of the reconcilers, would entrust the future of the Papacy itself to the good-will of the Italian democracy. To discuss these speculations would lead the present writer far beyond the purpose of this sketch. It is enough to say that they seem to be very far indeed from the eve of fulfilment. Men like M. Gambetta laugh at the Liberalism of such Catholics as M. de Montalembert and M. de Falloux, who in the last resort are as obedient to the Vatican as M. Veuillot himself. M. Veuillot, as we have said before, roundly asserts that a Liberal Catholic is no Catholic at all, and it must be confessed that the daily practice of his Church lends too much colour to this theory. She has no time to inquire what the Republic might do if it were suddenly to become Catholic. Is the Republic, it asks, hostile to the Church at this moment? Does the Republic seek to make education compulsory, and therefore secular? Does it debar the priests from giving the peasantry political commands when some one has to be sent to the Chamber of Deputies? Is it as favourable as a monarchy or an empire would be to the territorial claims of the Papacy? Is it more likely than a monarchy or an empire would be to lend an ear to those Radicals who, by stopping the salaries of the clergy, would give the last touch to the pillage of the Revolution? If the answer to such questions is unfavourable, the theological temper will prefer a military despotism to a reign of what it would call impiety. It is futile to wonder at such a choice, and to blame it would be unjust. As well might the raven be blamed for its note or the rattlesnake for its fangs.

It is not too much to say that all the deeper disputes of France are rooted in theological animosities. She is disturbed chiefly because the religious fervour of her people has been cast into the practical strifes of politics, instead of finding an outlet in the speculative controversies and the schisms of the Churches. Her parliamentary factions are sects rather than parties.

The machinery of the Government will never work smoothly until one or other of the two belligerent minorities shall have perished, or both have been softened by indifference. France will be as peaceful as England when her active minorities shall care as little as our own about the disputes which go down to the depths of society. Compromise, it has been said, is the soul of politics. It is equally true that indifference is the soul of compromise. But France is interesting as well as troublesome, because she is not a Gallio.

There could be worse things than the frank hostility of the Radical Republicans to the Church. Still worse would be a conspiracy of silence for the purpose of putting religion at the service of some unscrupulous saviour of society and his attendant gamblers in the Bourse. Nevertheless, an indescribably great and irreparable loss must fall on that country which has ceased to be fired by religious traditions and ideals. A nation cannot live on the glories of art, or the good bargains which are tabulated by Boards of Trade. A nation must pursue ideals and be animated by uncalculating enthusiasm, or it will soon become the stunted slave of its appetite for comfort and pleasure. Happily France lacks neither ideals nor enthusiasm. The political part of the community is stirred by the story of the Revolution, and by the glow of hope which centres in the Republic. The Republic, be it a Moloch or the symbol of beneficent rule, has already had as many martyrs as some religions. But, after all, the traditions of secular history can have no such purifying or ennobling influence as the deposit of spiritual life left by the great streams of Christianity. The examples of Robespierre and Danton are not quite so inspiring as the lives of St. Francis or St. Bernard. As we reflect on that fact, we must also think what might have been if priests and courts had not closed the avenues of rational devotion. It is bitter to remember what loss was inflicted on the political as well as the religious life of France when her Protestant communities were destroyed by massacre, by breach of solemn compacts, by an exodus of disastrous magnitude, by all the ages of persecution which make up the pathetic and awful records of the Huguenots. It is bitter to recall such lost possibilities in the midst of acrid impiety and unscrupulous fanaticism.

CHAPTER V.

REVIVAL OF THE LEGITIMIST MONARCHY.

One of the most interesting experiments in all the history of France was the attempt to revive a Legitimist monarchy amid the ruins left by the Revolution. The most brilliant nobility and the most powerful Church in Europe had been effaced. The most aristocratic of societies had been pulverised into untitled units by the tremendous roller of the Republic. And the Republic itself was gone; the Consulate was gone; the Empire was gone. The revolutionary names had become but memories; and a lonely rock in the Atlantic was about to be the prison, and was soon to be the grave, of the great man whose selfishness, and disdain for suffering, and passion for glory, were scarcely less wonderful than his mighty genius. But amid all this ruin the Revolution had left a form of society, bound together by instincts of equality, and planted on something like equality of inheritance. The Revolution had placed, not indeed the government, but what is incomparably more important, the social constitution, on foundations of adamant, and had given France a greater promise of stability in the future than any other country of Western Europe.

Such was the France which the Bourbons saw when they came back from their long exile in 1814, and a second time in 1815. It has been said that they were exactly the same when they returned as they had been when they went away, having "learned nothing and forgotten nothing" from the terrible calamities which had been largely brought about by their own folly. But that taunt is not quite true, so far at least as regards the new king, Louis XVIII. No one knew better how hopeless or how fatal would be any attempt to turn back the democratic stream, and build anew the whole of the ancient society. He was the cleverest and most cultivated man of his family. He used to study and write in the old days of Louis XV. when he was the Comte de Provence, when the most potent personage at the court was Madame Dubarry, and when none but philosophic dreamers feared a revolution. "You must put that question to the Comte de Provence," his - brother, the Duc de Berri, would say when he was asked about something within the compass of printed books. The Comte de Provence read much, and wrote pretty well for a prince. He wrote squibs against Turgot. He wrote plays at the old court; during his exile and after the Restoration he wrote an astonishing number of neatly-expressed letters. He was the polite letter-writer in person. And he was also as free from what some people call superstition and others belief as many an abbé of the old French Church. It was whispered that he was a Voltairean, and his favourite author was well known to be Horace. A cultivated man of the world, a cynic, and a cold voluptuary, he was a king in whom it is difficult even for the spirit of loyalty itself to find a hero. But he had a hard clear brain; he really saw some of the deeper meanings of the Revolution; and he was in no mood for tilting against the windmills of democracy, like his Quixotic brother and successor, the Comte d'Artois. So he gave his subjects the assurance of many liberties in the form of a charter or constitution.

At the same time no Bourbon was ever prouder of his lineage, or more tenacious of all the forms which expressed the majesty of the French throne. He never allowed even the obscurity and the privations of exile to lower the dignity of the phrases which befitted the head of the greatest family in Europe. When the Doge of Venice, at the bidding of Napoleon, had invited him to quit Verona in the darkest days of his fortunes, he proudly answered that he would leave the town, but that six names of his family must be erased from the golden book of the Venetian nobility, and he demanded the return of the sword which his ancestor, Henry IV., had presented to the Venetian Republic. When Napoleon promised to give him great territorial estates if he would surrender his claims to the French throne, he answered that, as the successor of Francis I., he wished, at least, to keep the power of saying: "*Nous avons tout perdu, fors l'honneur.*"

Such a prince was true to the character of a lifetime when, on coming to the Tuileries, he restored much of the stately pomp which had made Versailles the most brilliant court in Europe. Some of the greatest nobles in France actively performed such duties as seem to have a menial air when unsanctified by courts. The master of the household was the Duc d'Escars, whom the king called his *grand maître de la cuisine*. That great noble, it is said, had profoundly studied the art of cookery, was proud of the original genius with which he could minister to the subtleties of taste, and gave, it has been said, as much thought to the plan of a dinner as a great general would give to the plan of a campaign.* Another noble, M. de Cossé Brissac, had the direction of the *paneterie*. A third, the Comte de Rothe, was the king's chief cup-bearer. A fourth, the Marquis de Montdragon, had the honour of asking his Majesty what he would have for dinner. And the grand chamberlain of the king, the great noble who stood behind his chair at dinner, and who had the privilege of aiding him in the sacred mysteries of his toilette, was the ex-bishop, ex-revolutionist, ex-confiscator of the Church lands, ex-servant of the Directory, ex-spy, ex-Foreign Minister of

* " Histoire de la Restauration. Par un Homme d'Etat."
P. 233.

Napoleon, ex-betrayer of Napoleon, ex-ambassador at Vienna, ex-Foreign Minister of Louis XVIII. himself, ex-everything; the coldest heart and keenest tongue in Europe; the arch intriguer who had deserted every master that he had served, and who had still to desert another; whose vulpine sagacity took him more swiftly than an intellect like Bonaparte's, to the place where booty lay; whose life was one long incarnate refutation of the maxim that "honesty is the best policy;" the consummate diplomatist who had enriched himself with the pillage of commissions on the diplomatic work which he had done for his imperial master, and whose career was furrowed with lies; but who always told his falsehoods, and stole, and gave his benefactors up to the police, and got to the right side of the hedge, with the consummate grace and good-breeding of a *grand seigneur* of old France. No man ever lifted his hat so gracefully to the devil as M. de Talleyrand. He kept his place at the Tuileries chiefly for a reason which he himself expressed, when Louis XVIII. flattered him by asking how he had managed to trip up both the Directory and Napoleon. "*Mon Dieu, sire,*" he modestly replied, "*je n'ai rien fait pour cela. C'est quelque chose d'inexplicable que j'ai en moi, et qui porte malheur aux gouvernements qui me négligent.*" Accordingly the Bourbons did not neglect Talleyrand. But even he might have found his tenure of courtly office less secure if his skill in the courtier's art had not been equal to his disdain for the moral law. For at the Tuileries reigned much of that matchless ease, and dignity, and grace of manner which had been the chief distinction of Versailles. The court of the restored Bourbons was incomparably the finest school of ceremonial politeness in Europe. Perhaps our own may have been slightly like it in the days of the Stuarts. The courtiers had much of that composed serenity which enabled Talleyrand to bear in silence a shower of Napoleon's ferocious taunts, and then say to a companion as he limped downstairs: "What a pity it is that so great a man should be so badly bred."

The king and the princes of the blood showed for the monarchy and all its hierarchies a degree of devout respect such as humbler folk keep for the sanctities of religion. Louis XVIII. went through the ceremonies of the Tuileries, and uttered regal words of greeting to his courtiers, and presided at the council table, even when so paralysed by disease that he had to be wheeled about in a chair, and when his limbs were already stiffening into death. "A king of France dies, but he is never ill," was his reply to the entreaties of ministering affection a few days before the close. And the majesty of the courtly etiquette would not unbend even in the presence of death itself. One night the end came to the proud spirit of the old king; the public gardens of the Tuileries were filled with people watching for the token that he had passed away; couriers were ready to speed through France with the message that the people had a new master; the heralds were waiting in the ante-chambers for the summons to proclaim, "*Le Roi est mort! Vive le Roi!*" the courtiers were preparing to bend before their new sovereign; and, amid all these accompaniments of natural suspense, the king's brother and heir, the Comte d'Artois, his nephew and his niece, the Duc and the Duchesse d'Angoulême, knelt beside the bed of the dying monarch. After he had passed away, the new king, the new dauphin, and the new dauphiness rose to quit the room; and, as they were about to leave it, what was the first impulse of the religious, austere, sorrowful Duchesse d'Angoulême? It was a grand tribute to etiquette. Hitherto, as the daughter of Louis XVI., she had possessed the right of preceding her husband, who had only been the nephew of a king; but that right ceased from the moment at which his father inherited the throne; and, as the tearful group of mourners were about to go out of the room in which Louis lay dead, the duchess was the first to signify the change in her rank with the words: "*Passez, Monsieur le Dauphin.*" Nothing could bend the etiquette of Bourbon dignity. One may smile at such a worship of form, and wish for a little more naturalness. Some of us may say that the graces of Versailles and the Tuileries could have been learned only by making the little elegancies of speech and form more momentous than the larger things of public duty. Yet nations lose something when they give up, as they must do in the midst of modern hurry, the grand air of the old society. Life should be gracious as well as enlightened, the friction of unlimited competition should be eased by those courtesies which are the codified marks of self-respect or good-will, and we should ever keep in mind the civilising influence of dignity. Let us not forget that the old courts, if they spent our money and shed our blood without our leave, did teach us manners.

But the French court of the Restoration had to think of more serious things than deportment and the plenary inspiration of court circulars;

and, in truth, the social side of the Tuileries was of small account compared with the political. While Louis XVIII. was as nearly a Liberal as providential arrangements would allow a crowned Bourbon of the elder branch to be, his brother, the Comte d'Artois, had all the grand pretensions of the old court, which assumed that the rule of the Bourbons was cunningly interwoven with the final arrangements of the universe, and that a main purpose of the Christian revelation was to provide the kings of France with an apostolical succession of private chaplains. Of the Comte d'Artois it was really true that he had learned nothing and forgotten nothing from the calamities of exile. His stormy and pleasure-loving youth at Versailles had left him neither time nor taste for the studies and the society which had softened the inherited ideas of his elder brother, and made many of the young nobles disciples of Voltaire. He had hated the Revolution from the outset. He would not have given way one inch to Mirabeau and the other revolutionists who had come to Versailles, with insolent demands that the pinched common people should have some power of saying how far they might be fleeced for the benefit of the courtiers. He fancied that his brother, Louis XVI., might have died quietly in bed, and that there would have been no Revolution, and no Napoleon, and no upheaval of European society, if Mirabeau and other troublesome talkers had been locked up. A German is said to have reasoned in the same fashion about the source of the water in the Danube. The great river is said to rise in the pleasure-grounds of a gentleman in the Black Forest. On seeing the little bubbling spring, the countryman clapped his hat upon it, held back the water for a minute or two, and exclaimed: "Won't the people of Vienna be astonished at the stoppage of the Danube!" A great many political reasoners are like that profound rustic, and the Comte d'Artois was one of them. Hence, when the Bastile fell, and the court bowed before the democratic storm, he saw that France was no place for him, and he secretly quitted Versailles with his two sons, the Duc d'Angoulême and the Duc de Berry. Exile, the beheading of the king and the queen, the Reign of Terror, and the Empire, only deepened his hatred of all that was meant by the symbol of liberty, equality, and fraternity. Religious feelings gave in time a touch of spiritual fervour to his Bourbonic creed. A strange story is told to mark the turning-point of his life. His mistress, Madame de Polastron, when on a penitent deathbed, is said to have made him take the communion along with her, share with her one consecrated wafer, and vow, amid all the solemnity of the viaticum, that he would henceforth be true to her memory and live in the sight of the Church. He is believed to have kept his word. At all events, he felt bound by all the sanctities of religion to put down the revolutionary spirit, which had made the France of St. Louis set up the Goddess of Reason. But outwardly he was, when he returned to Paris, the same charming, gracious, lively being as he had been in the court of Marie Antoinette. He had the same vanity and love of applause; the same passion for the chase; the same fervent belief in the magical power of good breeding. He meant to conquer the people by his smiles and gestures and light words of courtesy. Sometimes he was compared to our own Prince Regent. As Thackeray has said, it was a matter of dispute which of the two princes was the first gentleman in Europe. Even the most patriotic loyalty must admit, however, that our own gracious prince would have stood the comparison better, if he had paid some slight heed to the imperative part of the twentieth chapter of Exodus, and possessed a trifling pinch of the virtues which could have been found among the least of his own lackeys. The Comte d'Artois at all events was a model of gracious courtesy, and when he entered Paris amid a crowd of the Royalists who had been waiting for the return of their old princes, he seemed to smile forgiveness even upon the agents of revolution. "*Plus de divisions: la paix et la France; je la revois enfin, et rien n'y est changé,*" he is reported to have said, "*si ce n'est qu'il s'y trouve un Français de plus.*" He never did utter these words; they were made up for him in the house of M. de Talleyrand, by M. Beugnot, a well-known Frenchman, who was set by the arch-master of deception to give a glowing account of the royal entry, and put into the prince's mouth some such *mot* as all Frenchmen could quote. "That is what Monsieur said," exclaimed Talleyrand, as soon as the words were read to him; "I will answer for him." So the phrase was put into the *Moniteur*. The French were delighted by the charming verbal grace of the heir to the crown; the prince himself never denied that he had spoken with a royal command of his native language, and I daresay that in time he as firmly fancied himself to be the author of Beugnot's *mot* as our own Prince Regent believed, in certain stages of convivial faith, that he had been at the battle of Waterloo. Nay, it is said that M. Beugnot, again at the prompting of Talleyrand, coined the almost equally famous boast with which Louis XVIII. is stated to have met the threat of the Prussians to blow up the bridge of Jena. The king was said to have declared that they would have to blow him into the air with it, for he would take his seat upon the emblem of the great French victory. That vaunt, it is said, was composed for him, or at least put into the concise form which would please the most literary nation in the world. The kings of France were as well served by the loyalty of wit as less favoured monarchs are by the mechanical loyalty of illuminations.

But the court soon found sterner work to do than dispensing smiles and accepting the paternity of foundling *mots*. The Comte d'Artois was sure that his brother was going the way of Louis XVI. by dabbling in constitutions. He had a true Bourbon contempt for that ministerial responsibility of which we in this country are so proud. He would govern as well as reign. He would command, and his ministers should obey. "I would rather saw wood," he said, "than be a king on the same conditions as the King of England."

At first the Comte d'Artois would not take that oath of constitutional fidelity which was exacted from all the peers and the deputies. Even his final consent was only of that reluctant kind which leaves a keen scent for the possibilities of evasion. Round him gathered a group of persons as convinced as himself that the only way to keep down the spirit of revolution was to revive the kingly temper which had enabled Louis XIV. to meet the Parliament of Paris with a riding switch in his hand. Among others was a princess, who is, perhaps, the most pathetic figure among all the courts of this century. Daughter of Louis XVI. and Marie Antoinette, the Duchesse d'Angoulême had been imprisoned with her parents in the Temple. Her father and mother and aunt had perished under the guillotine. Her brother, the dauphin, had died of cruel treatment in the revolutionary prison.

Already her cup of sorrow was so full that she had been called the Antigone of France. Grief had hardened her political ideas into austerity, and her strength of spirit would have made her a formidable power if her cousin and husband, the new dauphin, had ever reached the throne. Napoleon said that she was the only man of her family. Pity for her immense misfortunes and her really noble character was mingled with irritation at the stinging words which she threw at all who declined to be abjectly submissive to the throne and the Church. She was so sincere that, although a Bourbon, she often forgot to be polite. One day she was at the Tuileries when Charles X. was receiving the chief dignitaries of France, and among others the judges of the highest court of appeal in Paris. Those magistrates had deeply offended the king and his friends by giving a decision which asserted the freedom of the press, at a time when the court had tried to crush liberty of speech. When they came to make their bow to the Duchesse d'Angoulême, she made a quick gesture with her fan, and angrily said: "*Passez!*" The memory of such words lived longer than that of real injuries.

Round the duchess and her father-in-law, the Comte d'Artois, gathered many congenial spirits in that part of the Tuileries which was called the Pavillon Marsan. There was to be found a rival court to that of the king. It was a court composed in part of nobles who had once listened to the promptings of a passion for reform or change. Some of them may have spoken lightly of the clergy amid the fatal irreverence which, they thought, had ruined the monarchy. Some of them may have enjoyed the scoffing epigrams of Voltaire. Some may have chatted with courtiers who had gone to those select little atheistical supper parties, in one of which our own countryman, David Hume, found himself the most orthodox man in the room. But in exile all of them had learned to believe that the Church had been the very keystone of the social fabric which had borne the court and the aristocracy. It was the revolt against religious tradition, they were convinced, that had made peasant and artisan pull down the great hierarchy of social ranks which had been bound together by inherited beliefs, affection, and loyalty—in one word, by the mysterious cement of tradition. It was criticism divorced from the guidance of the Church, it was arrogant philosophy, it was impiety that had turned the French people against the rulers and the social superiors who had been set over them by Heaven. Thus many of the *émigrés*, as they were called, came to see in all forms of liberty so many kinds of revolt against divine order. Their hatred of Voltaireanism and of Liberalism gathered a religious intensity as they lived, poor and neglected, in the back streets of London, and it might be said that their mourning for the old lost gaiety of Versailles had something of Hebrew bitterness. A poet might say that they tuned their harps sadly to the strains of the Church, and that by the waters of our own Babylon they sat down and wept as they remembered the Zion of the Seine.

Men and women who came back in that temper were not inclined to tolerate either the manners or the claims of the masters who had grown up in France during their absence. So aristocratic a court as that of the Tuileries naturally disdained the plebeian nobles, whom Napoleon had lifted to the highest ranks of his brand-new peerage for their prowess on the battle-field. The smallest sprig of ancient nobility affected to look down on the rough soldiers whose fame had been carried to the ends of the earth by the victories of the Grand Army. In one case there is reason to believe that disdain did much to shape a great and memorable tragedy. When the emperor was banished to Elba, the most brilliant, if not the ablest, of all his commanders, Marshal Ney, naturally put his sword at the service of a court which had become the governing symbol of the nation. When the emperor broke away from Elba, Ney boasted to the king that he would bring Bonaparte back to Paris in a cage. But on leaving the capital to take command of the army, the marshal poured out a torrent of reproaches against the Bourbons. "I will not be humiliated!" he exclaimed to one of his old comrades. He bitterly complained that his wife came home to him with tears in her eyes, on account of the indignities to which she was subjected in the Tuileries; and he did not choose that the wife of Michael Ney, Marshal of France, Duc d'Elchingen, Prince de la Moskowa, the victor of Ulm and Friedland, the hero of the retreat from Moscow, "the bravest of the brave," should be insulted by the wives of nobles who were personally unfit to command a corporal's guard, and who owed their social position to an accident. He also complained that the king meant to set aside the generals of the Empire. "It is only with Bonaparte," he added, "that we can have consideration." Thus was Ney induced to betray his trust by going over to the side of Napoleon. The result was those Hundred Days of imperial power, which were cut short by the battle of Waterloo and the banishment of Napoleon to St. Helena. That Ney had committed a crime is indisputable; but excuses might be found in the conflict of authority in France; and at all events his comrades, as well as himself, believed that he was entitled to the benefit of an amnesty by the conditions on which Paris was surrendered to the allied armies. Even if he had not been sheltered, the king and the courtiers might have been expected to remember that Ney was among the greatest of Frenchmen, and that clemency peculiarly became Bourbons who had encouraged the enemies of their own country. But the courtiers said that Ney should die; the ladies of the palace were even more bitter than their husbands; the Duchesse d'Angoulême, sad to say, vehemently insisted that the marshal should be shot; Madame Ney passionately appealed to the Duke of Wellington, who only referred her to the king, and the king would speak no word of mercy. So Michael Ney died one morning under the balls of a firing-party in the gardens of the Luxembourg. He died as became "the bravest of the brave." And it would have been better for the Bourbons to have lost a great battle, than to have left such a memory of their inability to forgive a great foe.

The king equally refused to pardon another of the soldiers who had helped Napoleon, Colonel Labédoyère, in spite of the frantic entreaties of his wife. A civilian who had been convicted of the same crime, M. de Lavalette, was saved from death only by the romantic heroism of Madame de Lavalette, who went to his cell, changed clothes with him, and thus enabled him to escape. Many more — generals and officials—would have died if the king and his ministers had not at last resolutely set themselves against the avenging spirit of the courtiers. The most reckless of all judges and politicians are not ambitious kings, or even vapouring ministers, but the idlers of courts, the loafers in clubs, and the wealthy horse-jockeys, who shout appeals for the excitement of vengeance or war from the back benches to which they are banished by their own intellectual feebleness. The French ministers could show clemency at Paris, but they were not so well able to keep down the fury of the Royalists in the provinces. Thus was the Red Terror succeeded by the White. It is a sickening story of assassination and massacre. Violence, unhappily, is not confined to any one faction; reaction may leave as dark traces as revolution; and neither a courtly manner nor loyalty to kings is proof against the plebeian impulses of passion.

Among the party which gathered round the Comte d'Artois, and which thought that it was the last hope of the monarchy, the temper of intolerance was curiously stimulated by the spirit of theology. When the *émigrés* returned to France, they found that the religious character of their political creed was already embodied in an organisation which was to grow until it should almost overshadow the State itself. That was the famous Congregation. Many of us when we read the Republican journals of France, may wonder at the space which they give to the denunciation of the Clerical party or the Jesuits. In this country we are inclined to doubt the political sagacity of any member of Parliament who rises in his place to blame the Jesuits for anything that may happen to have gone wrong in Church or State. We have come to admit, in fact, that Jesuits are pretty much like other people, and even to suspect that Pascal did them some injustice in his "Lettres Écrites à un Provincial." We cannot understand, therefore, why one French statesman says, "*Le cléricalisme, c'est l'ennemi;*" why Prince Napoleon exclaimed, "*Semez le Jésuite, et moissonnez la révolte;*" or why so able a newspaper as *La République Française*, lately the organ of M. Gambetta, should spend columns in the denunciation of the political power of the French priests, who, in all the private relations of life, are really very good sort of people. We cannot understand these things, nor can we trace the causes which ruined the monarchy of the Restoration, unless we cast a glance at that mysterious, renowned, and hated Congregation, which the *émigrés* found budding into power when they returned to France.

When that country was blockaded during the wars of Napoleon, the Société des Missions Étrangères found itself nearly cut off from its old ground of work in pagan countries. So it turned its attention to the paganism of France. Soon there gathered round it many of those Royalist nobles who sincerely believe that the restoration of religion must go hand in hand with the restoration of monarchy. Placed under the authority of a Jesuit, the society was speedily organised with all the skill which never fails his great order. It had secret relations with all the departments of the State even in the time of the Empire; and it was enabled to become a great political as well as a religious power by the return of the king. Its aims were to overcome the still powerful Voltaireanism, to make the

French people loyal to the Crown, and to give to devotion to the Bourbons a religious fervour. In order to escape criticism it was organised as a secret society. A distinguished ecclesiastic was at the head of the order, and round him were gathered a group of trusted priests and laymen. The inner circle was scarcely ever reached except by men of the highest social station and unimpeachable devotion to the Church. Next came a much larger group of devotees who were going through the duties of a novitiate. These two groups were really the Congregation, and they secretly met in the Rue du Bac for religious worship and consultation on the political prosperity of the Church. In a looser way were affiliated a crowd of the men who held the highest posts in the court, the army, and the public service. Gradually indeed the Congregation included all the men who were at once intensely Catholic and intensely Legitimist. It is said to have included three members of the royal family, one prince outside that circle, two dukes, fifteen marquises, thirty-four counts, eight viscounts, twenty-one barons, and thirty-five chevaliers, beside a crowd of generals, judges, barristers, and deputies. They formed literary societies for the spreading of healthy doctrines; others for the delivery of lectures to the working people; and others, under the patronage of Saint Joseph, to help the industrial poor. Thus were loyalty to the Pope and the king, the cause of religion and of the Bourbons, divine duty and divine right, spread abroad in fly-sheets, insinuated in popular discourses, broadly taught in the pulpit, and doled out by charity organisation committees. The Congregation had its own wine-shops, the keepers of which had to see that their clients were loyal and religious as well as thirsty. The Congregation gave certificates of character to domestic servants, and thus turned itself into a register office for the propagation of the faith. The Congregation had enabled the Jesuits to come back to France under the shadow of courtly favour, although their presence was forbidden by law, and, under fanciful titles, they planted colleges to which all the great Catholic families sent their sons. The Congregation laid its hand on a vast number of the elementary schools by founding a half-clerical and celibate brotherhood of teachers, who are to this day the propagandists of Catholic doctrine in the class-rooms of the poor, and whom the Republican party is eager to drive from the communal schools. Perhaps the Congregation crowned its work by buying Mont Valérien. At that time Mont Valérien was merely a rounded eminence, and not, as it is now, a great fortress frowning in grim strength over the exquisite valley and beautiful windings of the Seine. A retreat was built on the top of that hill, and it took the form of a remarkably comfortable and decidedly expensive hotel, with a good billiard-room and a first-rate cellar. Thither rich penitents might go to profit by the counsel of the Jesuit fathers. If they sought to give special proofs of devotion to the Queen of Heaven, and therefore to the King of France, the strength of their obedience was tried by menial offices, and, when found sufficiently submissive, they reached that renowned company of devout and well-born Legitimists who were called *Jésuites à robe courte*.

But the chiefs of the Congregation were too shrewd to fancy that they could bring back the Catholicism and the loyalty of France by the hidden dictates of religious Carbonari. They knew that their sails must be filled by the wind of popular enthusiasm, and they systematically tried for years to preach the people into a great religious revival. Bands of eloquent priests went from town to town, and their coming was signalised by prodigious advertising. Known to be the favourites of the court, they were often escorted into a town by the prefect, the magistrates, the municipal officers, and the garrison of the place. The streets were lined with enthusiastic Royalists, who had been obliged to hide their loyalty in the dark days of the Empire and the Republic. White-robed priests and maidens wound through the streets in long processions, singing penitential psalms, and with them went men bearing huge wooden crosses, until they came to the spot in which the Revolution had planted one of its trees of liberty, and then —that symbol of destructive equality having been uprooted—the missionaries planted the symbol of salvation. In this case, unhappily, it was also a symbol of vengeance. The preachers lashed the hearers into a frenzy by sermons against the wickedness of the Revolution; the pathos of the Christian religion was made to find a centre in the prison of the Temple, its maledictions in the Convention; and the twin poles of piety and infamy were found in Louis XVI. and Robespierre. Towns often wore an ascetic air during the visits of the missionaries, and all the theatres were shut by order of the municipal authorities. A pulpit war was waged against books as well as principles and memories, for processions were formed to fling the works of Voltaire and Rousseau into a loyal bonfire in the chief square of the town.

Nor did the missionaries disdain to go for the stimulus of religious loyalty to the opera and the vaudeville, for, as some other revivalists have done, they often set hymns to lively secular airs, and sometimes they parodied in words of Catholic loyalty the songs of the Revolution. But there was one revolutionary song which they did not parody, and that was the song which had rung through Europe like the blast of a trumpet, carrying a sentence of doom to the enemies of liberty. It would not have been easy to attune the feeble words of sacerdotal loyalty to the fierce chant of the Marseillaise, nor well to awaken by its terrible music a host of accusing memories.

Such was the machinery of the mysterious society which had borrowed the devices of the Carbonari for the sake of the monarchy and the Church. It was very powerful, even though some of its devotees coolly denied that it had any existence. After a time the Congregation became supreme at the court. It guided the Ministry; it directed what professors should be appointed by the

Ministry; it made war upon the disloyal influence of science; it dictated to the magistracy; it laid its hand upon the army; it controlled the education of the young; and it had the honour of conducting the dynasty by the shortest way to ruin.

As a compact body the Congregation ceased to exist long ago, but the memory of its power envenoms the political contests of France to this hour, and helps to explain the popular hatred which defeated the Duc de Broglie's attempt to substitute himself and his Clerical friends for the Republican constitution. The Liberals naturally declared that the members of the Congregation were hypocrites. There were doubtless many hypocrites among them. It is not necessary to believe that all the Puritans were saints because they quoted the Book of Kings in the heat of fight, and wrestled in prayer when about to make a motion in Committee of the whole House. It is equally unnecessary to assume the absolute sincerity of judges who went regularly to mass when they found that the shortest cut to the higher courts lay through the sacristy. While Talleyrand was seen walking in a religious procession, it was impossible to forget the memorable occasion when, as Bishop of Autun, he had said mass at the fête of the federation on the Champ de Mars, in much the same leering fashion as Mephistopheles might have said it before Faust and Marguerite. But hypocrisy will account only for a small part of the power wielded by the Congregation. Hypocrisy will explain very little in the life of nations. Tartuffe has but a small diocese. Most members of the Congregation were undoubtedly sincere, and we cannot wonder that, believing what they did, they should have striven to plant the Church and the throne on the rock of absolute obedience to visible authority. But sincerity cannot overcome the infirmities of human nature, and when religion tries to put down impiety by political power, or when political power tries to keep up thrones and ministries by the help of bishops, the State is apt to become unctuous, the Church to become grimy, and both to become so unscrupulous as to shock worldlings. Nor can sincerity defeat those general tendencies which are to the moral world what the law of gravitation is to the physical. The Congregation could no more turn back that stream of general tendency which broke into foam in the Revolution, than the Society of Jesus could stem that kindred torrent which was signalised by the destructive force of the Reformation.

The missionaries were not France, nor was the Congregation, nor was the court, nor was the king. There was another and greater and more intelligent France, which gloried in the Revolution, ridiculed divine right, detested the Clerical party, and supported the monarchy only because it was constitutional. A distinguished visitor to the Tuileries could readily reach the centre of that other France, for he had only to cross the street and enter the Palais Royal. There he would have found another court, and the head of it was another Bourbon. If a Liberal, and especially if an intelligent Liberal, the visitor would have been cordially welcomed by a prince who had once been called the Duc de Valois, who at this time was styled the Duc d'Orléans, and who lives in history as King Louis Philippe. Descended from a younger son of Louis XIII., and also by the female side from a legitimised son of Louis XIV., he had a large share of Bourbon blood, and at least one of his sons, who is still alive—the Duc de Nemours—is a walking image of his great ancestor, Henry of Navarre. The son of that Duc d'Orléans who was called Égalité, who voted for the death of his kinsman, Louis XVI., and who yet perished on the revolutionary scaffold, Louis Philippe had been taught in early youth the philosophic precepts of the eighteenth century, had been among the first to welcome the glories of the Revolution, had attended the meetings of the Jacobin Club, and fought gallantly in the armies of liberty against the coalition of the kings. But the Reign of Terror frightened him away from the field of the Republic, and, flying from its vengeance, he had led for years a life of privation and adventure. He had taught mathematics under an assumed name in a Swiss boarding-school, he had visited America, wandered about Europe, and lived quietly at Twickenham, before the fall of the Empire had allowed him to return to France. He had made his peace with the elder Bourbons, in much the same way as some of his sons and his grandsons went a few years ago to Frohsdorf to pay homage to the Comte de Chambord. But Louis XVIII. never believed the conversion to be complete, and he signified his distrust both by denying his cousin the title of Royal Highness, and giving him merely the usufruct of the vast estates which had belonged to his family. The more generous Charles X. did, however, grant the coveted title, and the still more coveted fee-simple of the paternal possessions. Thus did the king minister to his kinsman's well-known passion for [making himself and his numerous family as comfortable as might be in this uncertain world.

Fondness for money was the chief blot on Louis Philippe's character, and it made him the theme of a thousand satires. After he had become King of the French, it once made him the subject of grave calumnies, when the poor old Duc de Bourbon, the last of the Princes of Condé, was found hanging dead from the window-cord of his bedroom; when suspicion fell upon a too well-known Englishwoman, the Duc de Bourbon's companion, Madame de Feuchères; and when it was found that by her persecutions he had been induced to leave part of his vast wealth to her, and by far the largest share of it to Louis Philippe's fourth son, the present Duc d'Aumale. But if Louis Philippe liked money better than became a prince, he also showed an unprincely and admirable respect for those homely virtues which are more important than thrones. He set a good example to the whole of France as a husband and a father. And his very faults had their political uses, for although his loyalty could be sycophantic at court, he happily found it easy to display a robust ingratitude at the call of political duty. As his personal interests were in the same line as those of France, he was fortunately able to show that, by forgetting the kindness of the king and listening to the voice of sheer selfishness, he could display the highest patriotism. A very clever, well-read, travelled man, a student of political history, sceptical rather than devout, fond of intellectual society, and skilled in discussion, he had naturally a contempt for the bigotry, the ignorance, and the political blindness of the court. Bluff and hearty, and yet wheedling in manner, he had always the air of a person who wants to sell something. He looked, in fact, like a princely, but advertising, commission agent, eager to dispose of a large stock of national happiness, and not unwilling to accept the usual percentage on the sale. He had admirable sons to offer to such great princesses as were in need of husbands. He was mortified because one of them, the Duc de Nemours, did not get a chance of marrying our own Queen; and he fancied that he had put another of them, the Duc de Montpensier, on the steps of the Spanish throne by that grimiest of all diplomatic intrigues which goes by the name of the Spanish Marriages. Nor did he forget that his father, and even he himself, had once been democratic chiefs; for he sent his sons to the public schools of Paris, and even after he had become the ruler of France, he was so ostentatiously a citizen king as to be fond of shaking hands with the least select of his subjects. But Heine maliciously said that he kept a glove for the purpose.

The Duke was more at home among the people who had learned politics out of books. They whispered in his ear that his countrymen would some day be glad to make a bargain with him, since he was to France what William of Orange had been to England. Their heads were full of our Whig revolution, and they could spin off at a moment's notice a parallel between James II. and Charles X. The Duc d'Orléans did not make a comparison between himself and "the glorious and immortal memory" of our own Dutch king, but he knew that such a comparison was made. He did not attack the court, but he allowed his attendants to say what they liked about its folly. He did not denounce the bigotry of the king, but he listened with virtuous encouragement when his visitors showed that it was again leading to the way of exile. Let it be said to his credit that he did warn the king in private of the fate which the monarchy was preparing for itself by allowing parliamentary majorities to be over-ridden by heralds and priests. But those who take their political opinions from heralds and priests are not to be checked by worldly wisdom. At last, then, when the court was obviously losing its sense of what was firm ground, and was said to be dancing on a volcano, the Duc d'Orléans put aside his airs of reticence and openly exclaimed, "*Au moins la faute n'est pas à moi; je n'aurai pas à me reprocher de n'avoir pas essayé d'ouvrir les yeux au roi. . . . Mais que voulez-vous? Rien n'est écouté; et Dieu sait où ils seront dans six mois! Mais,*" added the Duke, "*je sais bien où je serais. Dans tous les cas, ma famille et moi, nous restons dans ce palais. Quelque danger qu'il puisse y avoir, je ne bougerai pas d'ici. Je ne séparerai pas mon sort et celui de mes enfants du sort de mon pays.*" His sagacious and vigorous sister, Madame Adelaide, said the same thing during the Revolution of 1830, when she declared that the French might make either a king or a national guard of her brother, if they did not make him an exile.

Being determined to stay in France, whoever else might leave it, he naturally made himself agreeable to all who might be expected to remain after the king should go. Thus the Palais Royal threw open its doors to the members of the constitutional opposition, and to all the clever men who did not put their talent under the wing of the Church. If the chief judges of Paris were offended at the Tuileries by the scorn of the Duchesse d'Angoulême, they had only to cross the street to get a boisterous welcome from her Liberal cousin. If the orators of the Opposition were hooted in the Chamber, they were soothed and praised and petted in the drawing-rooms of the Palais Royal. Thither came those *Doctrinaires* who understood the British constitution, and prescribed its balm for all the woes of France. Thither came Benjamin Constant, the cleverest literary and parliamentary teacher of the sect; and Manuel, the best debater of the Liberal party, and General Foy, its most eloquent orator, and Casimir Perier, the great banker and statesman, who was to be the chief Minister of Louis Philippe, and Laffitte, the other great banker and political manager, who was to do more than any other man to give Louis Philippe a throne. The Palais Royal was a coterie of skilful Whigs, firmly convinced that they, and they alone, could "manage" France.

On going a little way farther from the Tuileries, and calling at the hospitable mansion of M. Laffitte himself, we should have found the same personages, mixed with younger, bolder, franker enemies of the Crown. You would have seen among others three men, who, each in his way, was to leave a profound mark on the history of France, and to be imperishably connected with her revolutions. One, who was made noticeable by his shrewd, sagacious face, was Béranger, the best political song-writer in the world. His light, airy, perfectly-finished verses had carried on the wings of music the praises of liberty, and of Napoleon, and of the Grand Army, along with satire of the court and the priests, to the homes of every artisan, peasant, shopkeeper, and man of culture. Such songs as *Octavie* and *Le Sacre de Charles le Simple* made him more formidable to the Bourbons than a whole heavy brigade of parliamentary debaters.

In the same room you would have seen the austere, haughty face of another man who, although still young, had already displayed commanding literary and political talents, who was for years to be the Prime Minister of Louis Philippe, and who, after pulling down the constitutional throne by his disdain for popular impulses, was to redeem many political errors by the green and revered old age which some of us have seen, and which all of us connect with the great name of M. Guizot. And there was a third personage, who died only a short time ago, and who is almost as well known in England as in France—a little, squat, restless, undignified figure; a round, spectacled face, blazing with vivacity, self-confidence, vanity, boundless curiosity, boundless talent; a young plebeian from Marseilles, who astonished everybody by his brilliant talk, and who, as Lamartine said, had sufficient gunpowder in his nature to blow up ten houses of Bourbon; the journalist who was pulling down the throne with the lever of his own maxim, that the king should reign, but not govern; the political leader who was soon to be the most prominent and the most mischievous minister in Europe; the historian who should afterwards debauch the minds of Frenchmen by writing the praises of Napoleon in twenty volumes; the patriot who was to learn political wisdom amid the gilded degradation of the second Empire; the great citizen and statesman who, chastened by the mighty misfortunes of his country, was, under the weight of eighty years, to leave a name which will be gratefully remembered by the latest generations of Frenchmen as the liberator of their territory and the first President of their Republic.

At the house of M. Laffitte and the palace of the Duc d'Orléans one would have met only the serious political natures, who, like M. Thiers and M. Guizot, had mastered the art of carrying motions in the Chamber of Deputies. All visionaries were coldly warned to be gone. But neither the Duc d'Orléans nor M. Laffitte could speak for the whole of that France which lay outside the court. One great relic of revolution still existed in M. de Lafayette, whose enthusiasm for the triumphs of 1789 had never been chilled even by the Reign of Terror, and who was still the same ardent, flighty Republican as he had been when he escorted Louis XVI. to the Tuileries. And there were many still more fervid Frenchmen, who thought that the promise of the millennium had been cut short by the fall of the Convention. There were men who, like Godefroy Cavaignac, found a religion in a Democratic Republic, and who would have gone as gladly to die as any martyr if they might thus plant such a Republic in France. There were not a few devotees of Napoleon who remembered nothing of the Empire but its glory. And outside these small minorities lay that great mute, mysterious mass of Frenchmen who had no political power. Nay, the qualification for the franchise was so high that some of the most eminent Frenchmen might, so late as the closing years of Louis Philippe's reign, have no votes if their wealth was not equal to their ability. One of these men, M. Cousin, on being asked for his vote by a candidate for a seat in the Chamber of Deputies, satirised the system in words of characteristic scorn: *"Monsieur, je suis professeur à la Faculté des Lettres, je suis membre de l'Académie des Sciences Morales et Politiques, je suis membre de l'Académie Française, je suis membre du Conseil Royal de l'Instruction Publique, je suis pair de France, j'ai été ministre, je puis le redevenir, mais je ne suis pas électeur."* Such a system could not last long in a country which has a greater respect than any other for purely intellectual distinction. Nor could the artisans and the peasantry long be denied political power in a land which more than any other is democratic. Universal suffrage was fated to come by the French love of political equality. We shall all of us do well to reflect on the meaning of that love. We sometimes hear that it springs from envy, which is said to be as much the vice of democracies as sycophancy is the vice of aristocratic countries. If such an explanation were true it would be very sad, because nothing can be clearer to any student of history than the fact that the growing and spreading love of equality is the master spirit of this age, and that sooner or later it will revolutionise every land in Europe. But the love of equality has, happily, a worthier root than envy. It comes from a rationalised sentiment of human dignity. It was against the sentiment of equality that the monarchy of the Restoration made war, by reviving as many as possible of the `old forms of kingly and aristocratic power. And against the cliff-like strength of that sentiment, the monarchy shattered the fabric of divine right for ever.

Charles X. found out the significance of that fact during the closing years of his reign, for in spite of the Congregation, and of his ceaseless attempts to pack the Chamber of Deputies, the Liberal majorities were constantly increasing. It became clear to him that if he did not put down the Parliament, the Parliament would put down him, by making him as dependent on Ministries as he supposed the King of England to be. He did make a small concession for a moment in allowing a cabinet to be formed by a liberalised Conservative, M. de Martignac. He sent for that eloquent deputy in much the same spirit as Marshal MacMahon sent for M. Jules Simon, and then he dismissed him as summarily as Marshal MacMahon sent off the equally eloquent Republican chief. His motto was, *j'y suis, j'y reste*. Resolving to assert his kingly power once for all, he summoned to the head of his council the Prince de Polignac, a less intelligent and more fatal Duc de Broglie. M. de Polignac was one of those gallant, honest, slightly-confused, polite, sincere, perfectly impracticable zealots, without whom no country would be complete, but who are more dangerous than the most hare-brained or unscrupulous dealer in the drugs of popular violence. Believing that the French Revolution had opened the doors of the nether pit, and that they might be opened again by Parliamentary majorities, he determined to keep them shut with the strong hand of kingly power. At the same time he meant to be perfectly loyal to the constitution, and he passionately assured his friends and his foes that he was an honest man. But he put himself on the slippery incline of personal government, and he forgot that a very slight movement, an involuntary step, the push of an enemy, the pull of a friend, might serve to make him illustrate the law which marks the momentum of falling bodies.

No sooner had he become Prime Minister, than everybody foresaw a struggle which might end in civil war. "Unhappy France! unhappy King!" was the prophetic exclamation of the *Journal des Débats*. The Chamber of Deputies made a memorable protest; the king answered by an equally memorable dissolution; and the country retorted by sending back a still more memorable majority of Liberals. Charles opened the session in a menacing speech; but it was noticed that, as he was about to step down from the throne, his hat fell off, and that it was picked up by the Duc d'Orléans, who returned it on bended knee. Bad omens go for much in a feverish atmosphere.

M. de Polignac tried, meanwhile, to charm the constituencies by the glories of a spirited foreign policy. Believing that France had been degraded by ignoble peace, and that the people were disgusted by the cowardice of past ministers, he wanted to change the map of Europe by the force of the Eastern Question. But, as the rulers of other lands were unwilling to hazard universal war, he resolved that, rather than waste the running force of military ambition, he should "drive into something cheap." So, taking advantage of a wretched little dispute with a wretched little potentate in Algeria, he fitted out a big expedition amid the sound of many trumpets, won a tremendous victory over his half-barbarous foe, and annexed the territory which he had invaded for the defence of French interests. But the Liberals and the great mass of the people refused to be pacified by the splendid possession which they had found on the other side of the Mediterranean. They wanted some homely rights, rather than the right to spend money and be despots among tribes whom most of them should never see. Another dissolution brought up an equally compact Liberal majority. So the king thought that the only way to "save society" was to make a *coup d'état*. Accordingly, at the Palace of St. Cloud, near Paris, after hearing mass on Sunday, the 25th of July, 1830 —a memorable day in the history of Europe— he and his ministers signed three famous ordinances — stopping the freedom of the press, dissolving a Chamber which had never met, and radically changing its composition. Had he any constitutional right to make these edicts? The Liberals said that he had not; but he appealed to an ambiguous clause in the charter.

There is, however, such a thing as political atmosphere, no less than political edicts. What a nation may languidly allow when its moral pulse is feeble, it will fight to stop when the iron of a sense of duty has entered into its soul.

That is what the king was now to find. When the ordinances were published on the morning of Monday, the 26th of July, they instantly threw Paris into a state of revolutionary turmoil. The chief journalists, with M. Thiers at their head, met and signed a famous declaration that they would not obey edicts which, they maintained, broke the pledges of the charter. A court of justice took occasion to affirm that the ordinances were illegal. When the police came to break, and thus stop, the printing-press of a rebellious journal, the manager confronted them with the criminal code in his hand, and warned the workman whom they employed that he was making himself liable to imprisonment with hard labour. M. Laffitte, M. Casimir Perier, M. Guizot, and the other leaders of the Opposition met with some vague and contradictory ideas of protesting or insisting. Scenting revolution, M. de Lafayette ran to Paris, and his great reputation gave a central figure to the party of resistance. All business was at a standstill; the manufacturers closed their doors and poured their workmen into the streets; the chief thoroughfares were thronged with an angry multitude; the students of the Polytechnic School broke out of bounds and offered to lead the people; the National Guards seized their weapons to protect their property; squadrons of dragoons tried to clear the streets; a shot went off near the Théâtre Français; the first blood was spilled; and the tempest of civil war was let loose. For three days did the capital ring with that terrible conflict which is commemorated by the proud column that now rises from the Place de la Bastile, in Paris.

Charles had no sooner signed the ordinances than he had gone to hunt at Rambouillet, but his attendants noticed that for once he was listless amid the pleasures of the chase, and that he allowed the stag to get away. His ill-luck in the forest was emblematic of his misfortunes in Paris. The number of troops in the capital was not sufficient to put down the crowds of armed Parisians—boys and old men, artisans and shopkeepers, and fashionably-dressed youths, grave fathers of families, barristers, young pupils of the military schools, and young students of law, among whom was, it is said, Jules Grévy, now the President of the French Republic. These volunteers fought with desperate courage. The troops had neither provisions, water, good guidance, nor the sense that right was on their side. It was clear that the victory would fall to the Parisians even before the Louvre was taken; it was clear that nothing could save the monarchy but the instant withdrawal of the ordinances and the dismissal of the Ministry; and the best friends of the throne sent one frantic message after another to St. Cloud, where Charles was staying. And what, meanwhile, was his Majesty doing, as the dull roar of the cannon was borne to the palace, as hundreds of brave men were dying in defence of his throne or of their own civil rights, as the courtiers formed silent and anxious groups, and as messengers came black with powder and half famished from the warring capital? His Majesty was playing whist! He was every inch a Bourbon. That rubber will remain among the sublimest examples of stately decorum in all the history of royal houses. Would it not have a grand air in a court circular along with a record of the taking of the Louvre?

Even Charles had to give way at last, and, roused from his bed on the night of Friday, the 30th of July, he signed a decree revoking the ordinances, and forming a Liberal Ministry. But it was too late. The Parisians were determined that he should never come back to the capital. Going to Rambouillet, he tried to save at least his dynasty. He himself abdicated on the 2nd of August. On the same day his unpopular but obedient son, the Duc d'Angoulême, renounced his rights as the heir. At the same time the throne was conferred on the king's young grandson, the Duc de Bordeaux, now known as the Comte de Chambord, and the Duc d'Orléans was appointed Lieutenant-General of the kingdom until the prince should come of age. All that was done on paper, but again it was too late. The Liberal Deputies passionately urged the Duc d'Orléans to accept the vacant throne in order to prevent the establishment of a Republic. Lafayette was won over to their side, and the Duc d'Orléans was styled the best of Republics. Talleyrand, the undertaker of every fallen government, sent the little message, *Qu'il accepte.* The duke, after a struggle with the claims of gratitude which he owed to Charles, did accept; the Chamber of Deputies proclaimed him King of the French, and the power of the grandest of all dynasties passed away for ever.

But Charles acted with kingly stateliness down to the very day when he left the soil of France for the last time. It was necessary that he should quit the country, and it was arranged that he should embark at Cherbourg. From his starting-point at Rambouillet to that port, the distance, as the crow flies, may be about one hundred and sixty or one hundred and seventy miles; but the ex-king went with royal slowness of pomp, and it took him almost a fortnight to reach the place of embarkation. He went, accompanied by his family, by the members of his household, by his guards, and by the commissioners of the new sovereign, who, in truth, were his only real protection. He went at a foot-pace, sometimes through pitying, and sometimes through sullen crowds; but he met with no insult, although most of the people would have lynched the Prince de Polignac and his colleagues. He was saved from injury by the popular comprehension of the maxim which he himself had denounced, that the king reigns, but does not govern. Perhaps the king's stately slowness was partially caused by a hope that Brittany and La Vendée would be fired by the memory of Charette and Cathélineau, and  would have time to strike for the throne of Saint Louis; but in the main it was doubtless a pure token of the king's respect for his office. One of his attendants was so shocked by the refusal of the people of Dreux to treat it with equal respect, that he went out of his mind. That was a beautifully sincere and complete expression of loyalty. At Laigle other attendants found that the king could not dine, because the hotel in which he lodged had only round tables, and no tables, therefore, of which his Majesty could take the head. But the democratic curves were speedily cut away by Royalist saws, and the extemporised rectangles allowed the king to dine without a fatal loss of dignity. The little fair-haired Duc de Bordeaux and his sister, meanwhile, added an infantile pathos to the wreck of royalty, for they had been taught to bow to the people in their better days, and, thinking that the procession to the coast was nothing more than a stately pageant, they cast their small smiling gestures among the crowd that lined the highway, and made tears start to the eyes of the rough Norman folk. Poor little remnants of a great dynasty, they were shedding their childish bounties for the last time among their own people. The Duchesse d'Angoulême, meanwhile, went with austere and silent grief, amid pitying enemies, on the way to her third and final exile. And the king, before parting with Louis Philippe's protecting commissioner, M. Odillon-Barrot, left a touching token of the political philosophy which had lured him to ruin. Speaking of the Revolution, he said: "I know all the threads of the conspiracy which has been woven. I could name the banker who has paid for the whole of the popular movement." That is to say, men had died by hundreds in the streets of Paris, and a throne had been flung down, our own first Reform Bill had been brought nearer to triumph, and Europe had been shaken from end to end, because M. Laffitte had flung about some gold! It would not be easy to find a more instructive comment in the whole range of courtly literature. Poor king! the influences which drove him out of France were atmospheric. They were the subtile product of the social wrong which had accumulated for centuries under his own family, of the revolt against the Church which had preached obedience to Bourbon commands, of the sceptical philosophy which was a revolt against spiritual tyranny, of his inability to understand the new time, and of the care for that common people to whom, we are finding, many of the most prized things must belong. Charles felt bound by motives of kingly and Catholic honour to cure those impulses of freedom which mean the impulses of human dignity. He was the best judge of his own honour. But the French were also the best judges of their own dignity; and there was no room in France for him and them.

CHAPTER VI.

THE LEGITIMISTS.

CLOSELY connected with the Clerical party are the Legitimists, a party which is the oldest in point of time, and certainly not the least worthy of respect.

They may be divided into two classes. First, there is the small sect who fill nearly the same place as the non-jurors of our own history. They demand the establishment of little less than the old monarchy, with the white flag for its symbol, and with the power of the king as unrestrained as it was before Louis XVI. yielded to the demands of the National Assembly. The king—such is the reasoning of the high Legitimists—may grant such rights to the Senate and the Chamber of Deputies as may commend themselves to his sovereign wisdom, and since Henry V. is an enlightened prince, he would grant as much liberty as would be good for France. But everything must come from his free will. If there should be another charter, it must be granted, not exacted. Although the king would not attempt to restore the old feudal rights, he would bring back with him all the personal power which perished in the Revolution of 1830.

Universal suffrage is in the eyes of the extreme Legitimists the very sacrament of infamy—the outward and visible sign of all the calamities which have befallen France. They may be excused for having no very tender feelings to lavish on what they call the rule of the mob, when the chief days in their historical calendar are days of mourning for a throne and a dynasty which fell by the hand of the populace. The taking of the Bastile, the slaughter of the Swiss Guards, the trial and the murder of the king and queen, the massacres of September, the tumbrels which carried loads of victims to the Place Louis XV., the dethronement of Charles X.—such, they think, are the results of that mob rule which is organised in the form of universal suffrage.

The religious Legitimists, as they may be rightly called, would make no compromise with the spirit of revolution. Their ideal is such a court as that of Louis XIV., freed of course from the profligacy which lay beneath the splendour of Versailles, but as Catholic and as ostentatiously observant of the old stiff etiquette as that of the Grand Monarque. The temper of the men who demand such a restoration is essentially theological in its disdain for the teachings of experience, its abhorrence of compromise, and its determination to import into political discussion the rigid dogmas which befit assemblies of divines. Practical men find it difficult to credit the sincerity of politicians who believe that the monarchy of France will ever be restored on such terms. They are apt to think that the Comte de Chambord and

THE LEGITIMISTS.

his devotees must be charlatans. But men of the world are not good judges of the political spirit which is nourished in solitude upon the legends of a Clerical loyalty. The religious Legitimists may say, that France has not yet seen the worst consequences of her departure from what they hold to be the one great principle of social stability. They may think that she will one day be sick of all the revolutionary expedients for curing the evils of revolution, and that, having tried republics, and military empires, and constitutional monarchies, she will go back to hereditary kingship. Or, even if they despair of such a day, they may feel a proud disdain for any compromise with false doctrine, and say that the issues of the future must be left in the hands of Providence.

The victory of the Legitimists, even for a single year, would doubtless be a great calamity. But let it not be forgotten that they have some political virtues with which society can ill afford to dispense, and which may be rudely nipped by the frost of democracy. Their loyalty even to a false ideal is better than no loyalty at all; their disdain for the vulgar promptings of self-interest is not to be lightly passed by, in these days of yearning for the bliss of heavy dividends; their readiness to fight for lost causes is better than the laborious waiting for Providence in the shape of parliamentary majorities; and, now that the restoration of their political power is happily impossible, some material for admiration may be found in the religious temper which they bring into politics.

Such are the high Legitimists. They may pair with those Bourbons of the Republic, who have forgotten nothing and learned nothing since they set forth the rights of man; who think that the chief break in the stream of French history was made, not when the monarchy was destroyed, but when the Convention overthrew Robespierre; and who would govern by the organisation of anarchy.

The ordinary Legitimists are not unlike the

very high Tories of our own country. While they do not say much about the divine right of the Comte de Chambord, they think that nothing can save France from a new series of convulsions but strict adherence to the principle that sovereign rule should be hereditary. They are strong Church and State men. They hate all forms of democracy. They would give as high honours and as much political power as they dared to the wearers of historic titles. They would try to restore or erect some form of political peerage which would do for France what the House of Lords does for England. Englishmen may naturally think that such a scheme would not be unwise. Some capacity for rule they might say will usually be found in any member of a family which has for generations or centuries been accustomed to make laws and wield power. Such a man will be guided by those incommunicable traditions and instincts of a governing class, which are laden with more practical wisdom than the most elaborate code of written laws. He will be free

M

from corruption, and he will always act in the spirit of a gentleman, because the dignified society to which he belongs can punish any breach of its canons with the tremendous force of banishment from its ranks. Hence it might be said that the chances of an aristocratic life would give a better Second Chamber than the choice of democratic units. I need not stop to ask whether that theory entirely agrees with experience. It is enough to say that France has no aristocracy like that of England. More than a century before 1789 the work of levelling had been commenced, and the Revolution finished what Richelieu had begun. A crowd of gentlemen still retain the titles of dukes, marquises, and counts, but they form a mere coterie, which is cut off from the rest of the nation by a spanless abyss of religious bigotry and hatred of democratic rule. Most of them live in the last century. Most of them have no aristocratic qualities, except personal gallantry and fine manners. Collectively, they are as imprudent as any set of men in Europe. To give them special legislative power would be suicidal. Thus nothing remains to break the even flow of that passion for equality which is natural to all civilised men, and which will grow with the spirit of human dignity.

CHAPTER VII.

THE ORLEANISTS.

SIDE by side with the Legitimists stands a party which was once the hope of France, which still represents much of her ability and moral worth, and which is interesting to Englishmen because it does them the honour of trying to import their constitution. I mean, of course, the Orleanists. They are the heirs of Mirabeau and the enlightened nobles, lawyers, and men of letters, who in 1789 sought by timely concessions to stem the tide of violence. They are also the heirs of the Girondists. Many political descendants of that interesting group were so dazzled by the splendid gifts and triumphs of Napoleon, that they consented to wear his livery. Most of them, nevertheless, still dreamed of a constitutional monarchy untainted by the vices either of military rule or of democracy. The fall of Napoleon brought to the throne a prince, who had been free at least from Clerical bigotry when he was the Comte de Provence. Louis XVIII., as has already been observed, was pretty well known to be a man of the world, a devotee of pleasure, and a Voltairean. It was also assumed that he would make his peace with the political and social spirit of the Revolution. In reality he had no such wish; but he was certainly more Liberal than the mob of nobles and priests who had lived abroad rather than submit to the rule of a usurper. He accepted, or, as the champions of Legitimacy would say, he granted, a constitution which, with all its defects, was an immeasurable advance on the despotism of the old monarchy. Still, neither the constitution itself nor the king's fondness for Voltaire could liberate the nation from the rule of nobles and priests, who had been hardened in their bigotry by the bitterness of exile. Even the faint gleam of Liberalism which came from the personal qualities of the sovereign faded away with the accession of his brother. Charles X. pitched his ideas of kingly prerogative as high as those of Louis XIV. himself. But the Revolution of 1830 seemed to bring the parliamentary Royalists to that promised land, which their leaders had seen only from the top of some distant Pisgah, while yet they wandered in the desert of opposition. The Constitutionalists had now their Joshua in the Duc d'Orléans, their captains of the host in Casimir Perier and Laffitte, their prophets in Guizot and Thiers, their fighting-men in the *bourgeoisie* to whom they entrusted the suffrage. At last, they thought they had entered into the possession of the Promised Land. But in truth the Promised Land was a mirage. The artisans, who did as much as the shopkeepers to fight the battles in the streets, found that Louis Philippe was very far indeed from being the best of all republics. They had exchanged the rule of the court for that of a middle class, as little disposed as any people to put trust in the Utopias of the faubourgs, and they discovered Louis Philippe to be as fond of personal power as Charles X. himself, although readier to use it for popular ends. He made boisterous attempts to win favour of the crowd, but they were defeated by the suspicion that he was very much of a hypocrite. At all events the Republican working men soon fell away from his government, if, indeed, they ever could have been counted among its supporters. Nor had the king any allies among that old Royalist party which had followed Louis XVIII. into captivity, and been faithful to him amid all the glories of the Empire. Louis Philippe had broken the Royalists into two camps by accepting the throne from the Revolutionists, instead of obeying the wish of Charles X. to become lieutenant-governor of the kingdom, and guardian of the young lineal heir, the Duc de Bordeaux, now the Comte de Chambord. Whilst the Liberal

Royalists went with the constitutional monarchy, the older and more enthusiastic supporters of the throne stood fast by the Legitimist king, and all attempts to close the breach between the two factions have failed. The only real supporters of Louis Philippe were the middle class, the shopkeepers, the crowd of officials who are on the side of every government, and the theorists, who had convinced themselves that it was possible to give France the blessings of the British constitution. The directing power lay with the small group of interesting and able men, who believed that they could thus transplant the most distinctively national, not to say provincial, among all forms of government. Unfortunately, many of them profoundly misunderstood the nature of the British constitution. They took the school-book theory that it is a balance of powers, represented by king, lords, and commons. Some of them seemed to fancy that it was a sort of cunningly-devised machine, which could be multiplied indefinitely by the skill of political engineers. The doctrinaires forgot that our form of government suits ourselves because it represents the collective feelings, wishes, ideas, and instincts, of a thousand years. But to establish the mere constitutional forms in another country might be ruinous, because they do not carry with them the thing itself. Our constitution is the most mysterious of all political products. Nobody can exactly define it. Roughly speaking, we may call it the rule of the most despotic elective body that the world has ever known. The drapery of the throne and the House of Lords are historical relics which hide the despotism of the House of Commons. No despotism, however, is absolute, and that of the Lower House is tempered by the friction of respect for a dynasty which is mastering the art of gracefully effacing itself, by the immense social power of an old landed aristocracy, by the subtle influence of an essentially aristocratic church, and by the tranquil Conservatism of the English people. France, on the other hand, has no such dynasty; she has no such aristocracy; she has no such church. All those agents of Conservatism were swept away for ever by her great revolution, and the unity of her people has yet to come. Thus all the traditional supports of her monarchical institutions having been cut away, her governments must rest on the broad level basis of democracy. The fact may be lamentable or not, but, at all events, it is one of those realities with which statesmen must count. An aristocracy, such as that which perished in the storm of the Revolution, can grow only in the twilight of feudalism, untended and almost unseen. It grows because it is the necessary link between separate clusters of humanity. And so also arise national churches. They likewise grow in the shadow, from little sproutings of piety, nourished by the social as well as religious needs of mankind, and watered by its benedictions. No one can tell when they first become great or powerful, and it is often difficult to say when they were established. We only know that when first established and endowed, they expressed the nation's highest sense of good. But such churches, or such aristocracies, if once pulled down, can no more be set up again than a thousand uprooted forest trees. Something may be put in their place, such as the Church of the Concordat, or a Second Chamber; but it is no more a church which the nation will obey, or an aristocracy which it will follow, than a thousand upright stakes are the original forest. The nobles of the Empire were flung down with contemptuous ease, and the Church of the Concordat hurts every dynasty that it seeks to serve.

The French admirers of the British constitution fail to observe that, if it is apparently the most successful of political fabrics, it is also the most delicate in its present form. It has never withstood the shock of such tempests as have swept over France. If England were to be agitated, as she has been already, and as she might be again, by controversies going down to the depths of national convictions; if the mysterious currents of the future should bring back such fervour as that which shook the land in the time of the Puritans; if sacerdotal castes were to become powerful as well as aggressive, and if the advancing spirit of equality should find political as well as economic disadvantages in the present distribution of the land—then, we may be sure, the constitution would be twisted into some new reality. Either the power of the Crown would be greatly increased, or the House of Commons would beat down the checks which usage still puts on the free play of its power. The constitution would then be more akin to that of an empire or a republic. It would have little likeness to the pretty thing of paper equipoises, which the Orleanists fashion in their studies and call parliamentary government.

It is quite true that the monarchy of Louis Philippe lasted for eighteen years. But the experiment was practicable only so long as the throne rested on a small body of obedient electors. The qualifications for the franchise was so high that it was held only by two hundred thousand people. So small a constituency could be "managed" by the skill of M. Guizot or M. Thiers. It could be "managed" through gifts of places, bribes, the influence of local magnates, and the pressure of public officials. There was never perhaps so corrupt an electoral body, Prudhon said, in his own savage way, that the king, a model husband and a model father, was "*naïvement, consciencieusement corrupteur.*" "*Louis Philippe, père de famille, sévère dans son intérieur, maître de lui-même, a fait un pacte avec l'enfer pour la damnation de son pays.*" M. Guizot, who was an austere puritan at home, and who has entered into a competition with Saint Augustine as a writer of religious meditations, raised many sneers to the lips of worldlings, not only by lending his hand to the infamous intrigue of the Spanish Marriages, but by allowing his subordinates to traffic in places for the sake of getting votes. His own hands, of course, were clean; no one spoke a whisper against his personal purity. But he seemed to have much practical sympathy with the advice which Pitt, in one of Landor's "Imaginary Conversations," gives to his young disciple Canning.

Pecuniary corruption was the very breath of life to the constitutional monarchy. The voters were bought as freely as if they had stood in the market-place. The system admirably suited the purpose of the little family party of princes and parliamentary chiefs who ruled the country. But it was as artificial and fleeting as the sand castles which a child builds on the edge of the advancing tide. When it was swept away by the democratic flood in 1848, a small knot of skilful doctrinaires found their occupation gone. Universal suffrage baffled the petty arts of intrigue, which had been found triumphant when France was like a close borough. In truth, the Orleanists say almost as hard things about it as the Legitimists themselves. Both regard it as a kind of terrible monster, guided by bad instincts, liable to fits of ungovernable passion, and strong with the strength of anarchy. "The people," some of them say, "is a wild beast, which must be tied down." To put it directly under the restraint . of the army might, they admit, be almost as bad as to leave it at large; at least a military empire would be scarcely less fatal to their hopes than a republic. They are not so chimerical; they fancy it could be disarmed by a multitude of artificial checks. They would tie the wild beast of democracy with such ropes of straw as electoral restrictions and Second Chambers. Such a process recalls the experience of Gulliver on his first arrival in Lilliput. After he had fallen asleep, his gigantic strength was no match for the ingenuity of the little creatures who discovered his monstrous bulk, and when he awoke he saw that he was bound by a multitude of threads, which, individually weak, were collectively as strong as a ship's cable. The sleeping Gulliver is the gigantic form of inert democracy, bound with the threads of a Second Chamber and a restrictive suffrage, and prevented from moving until he promises to obey the master spirit of Lilliput, the Duc de Broglie; who, at the distance of a few yards, can give the signal to bind or unloose the captive. The analogy is not quite reassuring. Gulliver was released on his own recognisances to keep the peace, and ultimately he ran away with the Lilliputian fleet. In France, democracy has always been able to wriggle out of such restrictions, and to run away with the aristocratic machinery.

If we look at the character of the theorists, who held that they could defy the French instincts of equality and transplant the British constitution, we shall easily see how and why they were misguided. It was not for want of study or ability. They were the most cultivated body of men in France. Although some of them had a proud lineage, they felt an honourable contempt for the ignorance which is said to mark some aristocracies. Many of them were distinguished writers of the second class. They filled most of the chairs in the French Academy; and indeed that eminent body was little more than a group of Orleanists for years after the fall of Louis Philippe. Since their existence as a party depended on their mastery of the art of parliamentary management, even their literary studies took more or less of a political turn. They sometimes seemed to think that the uses of history were exhausted when it had taught them to disarm the spirit of democracy, and they appeared to believe that the aim of political philosophy was to lead up to the throne of Louis Philippe. In the *Revue des Deux Mondes*, they lectured from an Olympian height on all the political institutions in the world. Perhaps their favourite text was the British constitution, and any one of them could have filled a professorial chair in the Sorbonne for the exposition of such of its mysteries as can be found in books. Some of them were admirable writers on the events of the day, and in the *Journal des Débats* they discussed political affairs with such well-bred ease and delicate irony, as the heavier pens of Englishmen have still to acquire. Many of the Orleanists were equally effective as parliamentary orators. If France could have been ruled by means of brilliant speeches and dainty epigrams, she would long ago have reached a haven of peace. Perhaps the devotees of the constitutional monarchy shone still more brightly in the drawing-room, when the talk turned on some political combination of last night or last century. They were the best talkers in Europe. They were matchless in their command over the resources of conversational strategy. Cromwell, Bolingbroke, and Voltaire were systematically routed over cups of tea. No people in the world knew so well the precise point at which their own Revolution had gone astray, and most of them, in truth, had written big or little books to show that it had gone straight to ruin when it turned aside from the principles of the British constitution. Their leaders were proud to be called Doctrinaires, and that name justly described their character, for they were men of books rather than of practice. They would have been great statesmen if they could have abolished three-fourths of human passions, and guided stormy nations by the tranquil mechanism of select committees. Being much too fine for this rough world, they mistook phrases for things, and their neat little constitutional philosophy was suddenly shattered by that unparliamentary mob with which they had forgotten to count.

Nobody, perhaps, was more surprised by the result than the chief schoolmaster of the Orleanist sect, M. Guizot. Nature and education had curiously fitted him to believe that half the evils of France could be removed by a cunningly-balanced mechanism. He was too able and far-seeing a man, it is true, to think that France could go back to the practice of feudalism or divine right. His fine philosophical understanding had been strengthened by the long and profound study which he had given to the early history of European civilisation, and his great book on that subject must be placed among the chief contributions to the literature of our time. Few Englishmen have been so well acquainted with the history of England. And he knew the political spirit of our country as well as it can be known by any mere literary student. He knew it so imperfectly, in other words, as to believe that the delicate fabric of the British constitution could be made to rest on the volcanic soil of France. His passionate love of order was, no doubt, rooted in the memory of his father, who perished on the scaffold amid the madness of the Revolution. Had he been a Catholic instead of a Protestant, his love of system and his domineering spirit would have given the Clerical party a fatally great chief. His ability and his temper would quickly have led it to destruction. Stiff and dogmatic, he was not made to be a successful party leader. Although his disposition was leavened by such Liberalism as he drew from Genevan doctrines and forms of church government, he was able nevertheless to leave a good deal of ruin behind him. Essentially a professor, before all things a lecturer, he lectured his country into revolution. His obstinate belief in the strength of a parliamentary system gave him the honour of destroying his master's throne; and the same strength of conviction was curiously shown in almost the last year of his life, when his trust in a hard theological creed made him bring the Protestant Church of France to the verge of disruption.

One of the most distinguished of the Orleanists is the present Duc de Broglie. In some ways the Duc de Broglie is a miniature copy of his great master. Lessen but do not destroy the philosophical understanding of M. Guizot; nourish it on the counsels of the Church and the subtilties of theology, the legends of ecclesiastical fancy and the casuistry of the confessional, more than on the harder facts of secular history; give it the curb of a Liberal Catholicism instead of a Conservative Protestantism, and we get the philosophical pedantry of M. de Broglie. Put infinite superciliousness in the place of that haughtiness which would have made Guizot lecture an angel on the discipline of heaven, and we find the equally rasping, but not so dignified, dictation of the Duc de Broglie. Both master and disciple are alike in disdain for small scruples. Personally pure, M. Guizot served himself with all the vast machinery of corruption which set in motion the constitutional monarchy; and his negotiation of the Spanish Marriages is made the more amazing by contrast with the beauty of his own family life. M. de Broglie is also a man of honour, and his friends say that he has a passionate belief in the goodness of parliamentary government; yet the trickery and the corruption of his ministerial career could not be matched in our time outside the range of Orleanist management. Perhaps he thinks that political corruption is made classic by the example of Walpole, who first eased the friction of party government by the lubrication of bribes. Perhaps it is merely a heritage from the constitutional monarchy. At all events, Louis Philippe was a sincere imitator of Walpole. He systematically assumed that convictions were for sale. The Duc de Broglie, it must be admitted, assumed that they must usually be stifled. Thus he shows that he is a pupil of the constitutional monarchy as well as of the emperor.

No description of the Orleanist party is complete without mentioning their great leader, M. Thiers.

M. Thiers was born in 1797, when the Revolution had already done the whole of its destructive work. The storm had swept away the grandest and most culpable of all European monarchies, the most brilliant, fascinating, and worst of all aristocracies, and the greatest, the most guilty, of all national churches. Louis XVI., Marie Antoinette, great nobles, beauties of the court, poets, philosophers, orators, statesmen, priests, had died under the guillotine. The remaining princes and most of the aristocracy were living in exile, plotting against the revolutionary government, and preparing for the restoration of the dynasty which Providence had appointed to rule over France. But, before the birth of Thiers, the destructive machinery of the Revolution had perished too. The nation had awakened from the dream of enthusiasm into which it had been cast by the Revolution. It had found that the hard facts of daily life—sorrow and suffering, vice and misery, poverty, ambition, and crime — would survive all declarations of the rights of man. But the army still obeyed the stimulus of a fervour which had made it more than a match for the whole of monarchical Europe, and, led by Napoleon, it had already astonished the world by the campaign in Italy. Victory had given France a master, whom fear of disorder and the loss of cherished illusions had made her but too ready to accept. In a little while the Republic was to be overthrown, and replaced by the greatest military despotism which the world had seen since the fall of imperial Rome. When M. Thiers was a child, Napoleon was carrying the eagles of France to half the capitals of Europe, and debauching the nation by deep draughts of military glory. He was reviving the forms of the old court with the addition of much tinsel splendour. A new aristocracy, mostly trained in the barrack-room, and bearing traces of that school of manners, was to take the place of nobles who were at least examples of consummate good breeding. A new church, under the orders of Napoleon, and largely the creature of his will, was to rise on the ruins of an institution which had given teachers and companions to kings.

Such was the France into which Thiers was born, in 1797. His birthplace was Marseilles, then, as now, one of the most fervidly political towns in France. On both sides his ancestry was remarkable. On that of his father, he came from an old family which had lived in Marseilles for many generations. His great-grandfather had been a rich and well-known merchant, who was ruined by an unlucky speculation. His grandfather was keeper of the archives of the municipality, and a man of literary culture. His father was a clever scapegrace, now a merchant, now an army contractor, now the manager of a travelling band of actors, now the lessee of gaming-tables, and again nothing in particular. He was always turning up in the wrong place, and he was usually in difficulties. Strange stories are told of his powers of talking about everything with perfect fluency, with absolute confidence, and with an interesting disdain for truth. He was by anticipation a caricature of his famous son. Although the family was Royalist, the father of Thiers was a partisan of the Revolution. I fear I must add that he was profoundly disreputable. At least he was a bad husband. He had deserted his wife at the time his son Adolphe was born. On the mother's side, M. Thiers came from a family of Greek origin. Thus perhaps a touch of Levantine vivacity and shrewdness was added to the kindred qualities which he had inherited from his Provençal blood.

His maternal grandmother, a Madame Amie, was the aunt of André Chenier, the poet, who added imperishable things to the literature of the Revolution, and who perished on the scaffold when the madness of the Reign of Terror smote down the Girondists. When mounting to the guillotine, "To die so young!" he exclaimed; and then, striking his forehead, he said: "There was something there."

Madame Thiers and the whole of her family were Royalists. Had her son followed her counsel, he would, in the most important periods of his life, have been a partisan of the Comte de Chambord and the white flag. She was a devoted mother. Deserted by her worthless husband, and dependent on her own family for bread, she gave herself up to the education of her boy. Through the influence of her cousin, Joseph Chenier, the brother of the poet, she got for him one of those scholarships which Napoleon had established in the public schools of France. Thus Thiers was, in a way, indebted for his education to the man whose marvellous history he was afterwards to write. At the Lycée, or high school, of Marseilles, Thiers was as bright and vivacious as in after life. As in after life, too, he displayed strong military tastes, devoting himself especially to studies, such as mathematics and history, which would fit him to be a soldier. Indeed, the style of education in the public schools was largely military, in order to give Napoleon a constant supply of instructed officers. The scholars were fed on the stories of the great imperial victories. Austerlitz and Jena had been won shortly before Thiers went to college as a lad of eleven, and when he was there, the *Moniteur* brought the chequered story of the Peninsular War. It told also of the invasion of Russia, the tremendous battle of Borodino, the burning of Moscow, the awful retreat to the borders of Poland. It described the emperor's vain efforts to make head against the coalition of Europe, his abdication, his exile to Elba, his triumphant return to France. It recounted the crowning judgment of Waterloo, and the expiation of St. Helena. It is difficult for this generation to call up, by any effort of imagination, the fever in which the youth of France were kept in that season of victory, defeat, invasion, with the empire of the world for the prize, and the restoration of an odious dynasty for the penalty of failure. It was a time such as comes only once in centuries, and to the latest hour of his life Thiers bore the mark of its exciting lessons.

The year before Waterloo put an end to his career at school and also to all his hopes of entering the army; the Bourbons, who had now returned to France, sought only aristocratic officers. His mother did not know what to do with her brilliant son, and the number of available careers was sadly limited by her poverty, which was such that she had to eke out a living by her needle. At one time she thought of putting her boy into a merchant's office. But she was too intelligent not to see his wonderful talents, and not to sympathise with his ambitious hopes. Her own mother, who lived with her and had also become poor, was devoted to the young boy, and by the sale of a little property she got the funds requisite for making him a barrister. The whole family went to the town of Aix, which was the seat of a law school. Aix had long had its provincial gentry and its lawyers of repute. The same families had lived there for generations. The society was cultivated, and its tastes literary. There was a literary academy as well as courts of justice. Thiers, who was eighteen years old when he went to Aix, soon became the best-known young man in the town. He studied little law, but he read widely in history and literature.

Then, as in after life, he had amazing power of talk. He would speak for hours about art, literature, politics, military tactics, religion, philosophy, finance—anything that came in his way. Rich cultivated people invited him to their houses, and were delighted by his intellectual brilliancy, as well as amused by his boundless self-confidence. The more Conservative families, on the other hand, were shocked by the freedom of his Liberalism. "He writes well," they said, "but he thinks badly." Among the lads of his own age, he was an intellectual leader, and even then he had boundless ambition and confidence in his own powers. The career of Napoleon seemed to make anything possible to a gifted young man, and Thiers was already bent on governing France. "We shall see when we shall be ministers," he used to say to his fellow-students. At that time, he gained his first literary distinction. The Academy of Aix had offered a prize of twenty pounds for the best essay on the life of the great moralist, Vauvenargues, who had lived in the neighbourhood. Thiers, among others, handed in an essay, and it was by far the best. It was unsigned, of course, but it was accompanied by a sealed envelope containing his name. Without breaking the envelope, the judges learned the secret of the authorship, and some of them were too Conservative to like his defiant Liberalism. They did not dare to give his essay a second place, but they made a compromise by declining to award any prize, and inviting a second competition. Thiers was more than a match for their craft. Writing, in hot haste, another essay on the same subject, he sent it to a friend in Paris, who reposted it to Aix. The members of the academy were delighted to see from the post-mark that such notice of their academy had been taken in the capital, and they were far more delighted to find the essay so good as to merit the prize. So they gave the first place to it, and the second to the essay of Thiers. When they opened the envelopes containing the names of the writers, they found that the first as well as the second essay had been written by their troublesome young townsman. The essay merited a prize, if I may judge from the only passage of it which ever seems to have been published. It was a bright, lively production, and it contains one saying that may be taken as the motto of its author's life. "Since man," he said, "has been created for action, the more he acts the more he fulfils his destiny." Such, at least, was the belief on which Thiers shaped his career. A less contemplative nature never lived; he did not understand day-dreaming; he was consumed with a passion for work; and at the age of eighty he worked harder than most men can do at the age of thirty or twenty-five.

The writing of the essay on Vauvenargues determined the immediate future of Thiers. The most intimate of his friends at Aix was a young man, a year older than himself, who was to be bound to him through life by a tie of beautiful devotion, who was also to earn an illustrious name, and who still lives amid the respect and admiration of France—M. Mignet, the distinguished historian, and perpetual secretary of the French Academy.

Mignet had already gone to Paris, and he had won a prize of sixty pounds offered by the French Academy for the best essay on the institutions of St. Louis. It was he who put Thiers's essay on Vauvenargues in the post for Aix. Fired by the example of Mignet, Thiers also went to Paris, carrying with him the twenty pounds which he himself had won, and he made his way to the very humble lodgings of his friend, who had already found congenial work as a writer for the *Courrier de France,* to which he contributed articles on foreign politics.

Here let me say something about the state of France and Paris in 1821, the year in which Thiers came to the capital. The court, the nobles, and the clergy were all back. They were more bigoted than they had been before the Revolution, because they had taught themselves to believe that the throne would never have perished, and they themselves would never have been exiled, if they had not trifled with the spirit of philosophical inquiry, and bent before the mob. Democracy had become formidable, they thought, because they had not gone zealously to mass, because they had allowed Voltaireanism to sneer away the sanctity of the priesthood, because many of them had courted the society of brilliant sceptics like Diderot, because they had forgotten that the Church was the mainstay of social order. The king and the queen had been beheaded because concessions had been made to what was called the spirit of reform. The States-General ought to have been shut up when the deputies became insolent; Mirabeau should have been made to cool his ardour in prison; and the mob of Paris should have been shot down before it was insolent enough to attack the Bastile. Thus would France have been saved from the scourge of Robespierre and Danton, from the Reign of Terror, from the wars of the Empire. Rough old soldiers of the Empire learned the forms and the phrases of devoutness, the chaplains of the regiments were potent masters of promotion, and the dignity of the Church was protected by laws of atrocious severity against sacrilege. The court could not indeed undo the rough work of the Revolution by reviving the law of primogeniture, or by giving exclusive rights of State pay to the Catholic Church. So far, the fruits of the Revolution were guarded by the Charter or Constitution which had been signed by Louis XVIII. But the charter gave the suffrage to a very small class of the community, it restricted the choice of deputies, and the court did all in its power to fritter even that little Magna Charta away. The courtiers said that the king had "granted" it of his own free will, thus implying that what he had given he could take away.

Such was the court down to 1830; and the picture has a more than historical interest. But outside the court was the real Paris, that wonderful centre of intellectual life, to which we can find no parallel nearer than mediæval

Florence or ancient Athens. The rich middle class was full of ambition and of hope. It wanted to establish a real parliamentary government, which should perpetuate the freedom without the follies of the Revolution. It wanted a parliamentary and constitutional monarchy. It despised the divine right of kings as much as it detested the rule of priests, and the French love of equality was cut to the quick by the pretensions of the patrician families. The political feelings, and hopes, and beliefs of this class were expressed by Béranger, whose light, airy, perfectly-finished verses seem still to be the very voice of pleasure-loving, brilliant, intellectual, democratic, sceptical Paris. The cultivated classes had a great Conservative leader in Casimir Perier, and the Liberals had a less great but more amiable chief in M. Laffitte. M. Talleyrand was still vigorous, and he made war on the court in his scoffing epigrams. At the same time, there was a wonderful outburst of literary and intellectual power. Never, in fact, has the literary genius of France been more brilliant since the days of Louis Quatorze, Chateaubriand, Benjamin Constant, Paul Louis Courier, Lamartine, Lamennais, Victor Hugo, Guizot, Villemain, Cousin, Saint Beuve, Alfred de Vignet; all these men, and many others, were already pouring out prose and poetry, philosophy, criticism, political dissertation. Even when nominally on the side of the court, they were making Liberal ideas spring up by the mere stimulus which they gave to thought. The working classes were less of a power, for they had not yet received the suffrage, nor had the cause of that Republic, to which they still fondly clung, been freed from the stains of blood with which it had been splashed by the Reign of Terror. Nor again had they yet any considerable leader except in Lafayette, the remaining hero of the Revolution. The triumph of the Republic had yet to come.

Such was the Paris to which Thiers came in 1821, in which he was soon to exercise a profound influence. The beginning of his splendid career in the capital was very humble. He went to live in the same abode as his friend Mignet. His chamber was in the fourth floor of a dingy house in the Passage Montesquieu, which is situated in one of the most noisy and populous quarters of Paris. The furniture of the room, as it is described by an eye-witness, was composed of a modest chest of drawers and a wooden bed, two chairs, and a rickety black table. A few books lay at hand, and the only ornament was a bad engraving of Madame de Staël's heroine, Corinne. In little more than ten years the occupant of that poor little room was to live in one of the mansions which are allotted to the ministers of state.

But Thiers can never be said to have had a battle with real poverty, for he began to be successful only three weeks after he came to Paris. Partly from necessity and partly from choice, he flung himself into a career for which he had consummate aptitude, and which at that time was the strongest road to power in France. He became a journalist. Introduced to the editor of the *Constitutionnel*, which was then the chief organ of public opinion, he was at first set to the task of writing articles on art. He happened to be peculiarly well qualified for that work. In the houses of his rich and cultivated friends at Aix he had studied paintings, etchings, statues, medals, many of which were the spoils of Napoleon's campaigns. He was passionately fond of art. He could paint with some skill, and one of the first things he did on coming to Paris was to visit the great galleries. At last he was entrusted with political writing, and he speedily became the first political writer of a country which has a genius for discussion. Compared with the great Parisian journals of our own day, not to speak of others nearer home, those to which Thiers contributed were, it is true, unimportant. The *Constitutionnel* was a small sheet of four pages, and the leading articles were short and fragmentary. But the character of the writing improved as the struggle with the court became more dangerous.

In order to get the power of directing the *Constitutionnel,* Thiers bought a share in it with money borrowed from a friend. On the eve of 1830, when the combat was becoming critical, and when the proprietors of the *Constitutionnel* would not permit him to risk the safety of a valuable property by sufficiently bold writing, he founded another journal in concert with his friend Mignet and Armand Carrel, who was afterwards to become even a greater political writer than himself. That journal was the famous *National,* which powerfully helped to pull down the throne of Charles X. Thiers's articles were often made masterpieces of political writing by the closeness of their argument, the perfect lucidity of their style, the aptness and brilliancy of their illustrations. Take this one example of the manner in which he shows the superiority of representative over despotic government. "It also has its Cæsars, but they are Chathams, Pitts, and

Cannings. They come at the head, not of armies, but of majorities. We do not assassinate them; we send them to the House of Lords." In another article in the *National*, Thiers laid down the famous maxim, borrowed from the practice of our own constitution: "*Le roi règne et ne gouverne pas!*" Thiers's articles supplied not only political instruction, but the pithy maxims which are the current coin of political reflection. The writing of his leading articles would have given ample work to an able man of ordinary strength. But Thiers was a prodigy of physical endurance as well as mental activity, and he speedily set himself to write the history of the great Revolution. That book, which he published in monthly parts, made him famous. After a short time of neglect, the Parisians, or rather the French people, read it with profound interest. It was sold by thousands. People were fascinated by the charm of the narrative, rapid, lucid, full of incidents and glowing with bright intelligence. They began to discuss once more the crimes of that old monarchy which Charles X. and his courtiers sought to revive. They were reminded of what could be said in favour even of Robespierre himself. They were taken once more over those battlefields of the Republic which the later military glories of the Empire had been permitted to obscure. Thus Thiers, by writing his history of the Revolution, did much to produce that change of feeling which brought on the Revolution of 1830. Nor did even the writing of the history exhaust his activity. He deliberately tried to become an accomplished man of the world, a feat made difficult by many physical defects. He was scarcely five feet high, and his figure was short, squat, and ungraceful. The nearness of his sight obliged him to use spectacles, and the bright intelligence of his square compact face was set off by no grace of feature. His voice was shrill, and he spoke with a southern accent, amusing to fastidious Parisian ears. His gestures were awkward, incessant, almost grotesque. He was absolutely wanting in that repose and ease of manner which form the crowning grace of good breeding. Yet he overcame many of these defects by laborious attention to the small as well as to the great accomplishments of life. He made himself a good rider at the expense of some falls, and also of acquaintance with men whose talk was of nothing but horses. He dined out a great deal. He frequented those cafés which are the clubs of the Parisians, and astonished people by the abundance and eloquence of his talk on every subject under the sun. He was to be seen night after night in the drawing-room of M. Laffitte, gesticulating, declaiming, denouncing the Government, pouring out epigrams, explaining the details of finance, dogmatising about the mysteries of military strategy, or discussing the artistic monuments of the Renaissance. Talleyrand, the shrewdest spirit of the time, predicted that he would become great; and made him the subject of one of his *mots*. Thiers, he said, is not a *parvenu*; he is an *arrivé*. There was also a touch of romance in his career at this time, for he had to fight a duel with the father of a young lady at Aix whom he was said to have jilted, and he was nearly shot. He became, in short, one of the best-known men in Paris.

He happened to dine one night at a restaurant in the Palais Royal in company with Lamartine, who was then on the side of the Bourbons; and the poet has left a brilliant, if rather sarcastic, picture of the young journalist. Perhaps, he hints, Thiers, being full of southern heat, had too good an opinion of his own abilities. "Modesty," demurely adds Lamartine, "is a northern virtue, or an exquisite fruit of education. Thiers spoke first, he spoke last, he scarcely listened to what was said in reply, but he spoke with a justice, an audacity, a fertility of ideas, which made it easy to pardon the volubility of his lips. . . . He had enough of gunpowder in his nature to blow up ten governments. I went away," says Lamartine, "more than ever convinced that the monarchy was doomed because it had pleased Providence to give it such an enemy."

Such was Thiers on the eve of 1830. Charles X. had made what he called a last concession to the Liberals by giving the place of Prime Minister to M. de Martignac, one of the most illustrious men that ever adorned the French bar; a cultivated, gentle, noble spirit, endowed with a flowing and persuasive eloquence which, in some of its higher notes, recalled the grand declamation of the most gifted of the Girondists, Vergniaud. But it was not intended that M. de Martignac should succeed, and a trivial check on the subject of a petty municipal bill sufficed to throw him from power. The king then gave his confidence to the Prince de Polignac, who was the ambassador in England, who had studied our institutions and could talk glibly about the British constitution; who admired our Tory party, and thought that the Duke of Wellington was a great statesman, but who hated liberty with an inexpressible hatred; who was a fanatic in the cause alike of Absolutism and Catholicism; who was convinced that Liberalism meant anarchy, and that the art of government was summed up in the devices of intrigue and the word of command; who had no fear because he saw no consequences, and who strung all these qualities together by a serene, unchangeable, smug, smiling faith in the goodness of his own intentions.

Before the appointment of the Prince de Polignac, Thiers had intended to accompany Captain La Place in a naval expedition round the globe, with the object of getting materials for a general history of the world. That was one of the many objects which his bright restless brain took up and threw away. But the Ministry of the Prince de Polignac was, he knew, a signal for war to the knife against the constitution, and the herald of a *coup d'état*. Thiers, who was essentially a journalist and a political leader, felt that he had more important work to do in Paris than he could find in the South Seas. He stayed at home, and, by doing so, he helped to overthrow the monarchy. The time for action soon came, for the Chamber of Deputies passed a vote of no confidence in the Ministry, and expressed its condemnation in a celebrated address to the king himself, signed by two hundred and twenty-one deputies. The king answered by dissolving the Chamber, and the country answered by re-electing the two hundred and twenty-one deputies. Still the king would not submit. He appealed to his honour, to his sovereign right, to his good intention, to his duties. He refused to accept the dilemma either of *se démettre* or *se soumettre*. He was encouraged by the Prince de Polignac, who declared that order, property, and religion were all at stake; that war to the death must be waged against latent Radicalism; that the contest lay between the king and the Gambettas of the period. Nor did the king and his ministers content themselves with mere protests, for, stepping beyond the limits of the constitution, they, on the 26th July, suspended the freedom of the press, and decreed a second dissolution by the famous ordinances, which were mere records of the king's personal will. But the king and his ministers did not know the political temper with which they had to deal. I daresay they never gave a thought to the fiery young political leader, who had sufficient gunpowder in his mind to blow up ten Bourbon governments. Instead of obeying the illegal decrees, M. Thiers made them the subject of a protest, which may rank with the most memorable acts of all his life. Calling a meeting of his fellow-journalists at the office of the *National*, he insisted that they should publicly and collectively refuse to obey the ordinances. Some of them were too timid to follow him. While they were resisting his fiery gesticulation, his young friend and fellow-journalist, M. de Rémusat, came into the office, and Thiers said to him: "We must not submit to the ordinances; we

P

must oppose them by an act. Will you sign the protest?" The young aristocratic man of letters instantly said that he would, and the doubting spirits followed his example. Then Thiers drew up the famous refusal to obey the ordinances, and it was signed by himself, Mignet, Armand Carrel, De Rémusat, and the chief political writers of France. That document is the Magna Charta of French journalism, and it gave the signal for the Revolution of 1830. It was signed on the 27th July, little more than twenty-four hours after the appearance of the illegal decrees, and on the same day barricades arose throughout Paris. The ministers had, meanwhile, been living in such a fool's paradise that they had not thought it needful to fill Paris with troops. The king and the court were at St. Cloud, a few miles from the capital, and Charles, as I have said elsewhere, quietly spent his evenings at the card-table. He smiled blandly now and then when he heard that the insurrection was spreading. Polignac, who was also at

St. Cloud, was equally infatuated. Hearing that some of the troops would not fire on the people, he said: "Then we must fire on the troops." But the rebellion spread from hour to hour; the soldiers had neither food nor ammunition, and many of them joined the defenders of the barricades. The Louvre was taken by assault, and the soldiers were driven from the Tuileries. The contest was no longer a revolt, it was a revolution. A few days after the publication of the ordinances, Charles X. had to fly to Rambouillet. In two days more he abdicated in favour of his young grandson, the Duc de Bordeaux, now known as the Comte de Chambord. Immediately afterwards he took his way to England, the great harbour of refuge for the victims of regal infatuation. Thus disappeared from France the last legitimate representative of the most illustrious of all European dynasties.

Meanwhile Thiers had displayed even more than his usual activity, and had given a decisive turn to the Revolution. The leaders of it had three courses before them. They could try to establish a republic, or allow the Duc de Bordeaux to take the place of his grandfather, or finally give the throne to the king's cousin, the Duc d'Orléans, better known as Louis Philippe. M. de Lafayette was in favour of a republic, and the young enthusiastic partisans of that cause had already seized the Hôtel de Ville, the civic symbol of French sovereignty. But Thiers, Guizot, Casimir Perier, Laffitte, and the more responsible leaders of the Revolution had inherited a distrust of a republic, and there can be little doubt that the time had not yet come for setting up such a government. Thiers himself had audaciously tried to close the controversy, by rushing away to Neuilly, the residence of the Duc d'Orléans, and beseeching him to be the William III. of France. His journey was a curious freak of audacity, for he had to ride through barricades manned by Republicans, and in order to reach the gates of the château he had almost to ride for his life. Even when he got there, it needed, in a young political writer, a good deal of courage—some people would say a good deal of impudence—to offer the throne of France with no other warrant than that of a little meeting held in the Rue de la Ville l'Évêque. At first the mission threatened to be a failure, for Louis Philippe himself was not at home, or at least he was conveniently invisible, and his pious decorous wife, Marie Amélie, was shocked by the proposal to betray a king who had covered her husband with kindness. But Louis Philippe's sister, Madame Adelaide, was made of more ambitious stuff. She was one of those women who have played a great part in the strifes of France, and she instantly declared that her brother would accept the throne. Meanwhile, the king had tried to tie the hands of the Duc d'Orléans, by appointing him the guardian of the Duc de Bordeaux and lieutenant-governor of the kingdom. Had that position been accepted, it would possibly have been well for France, as the

Royalist party would have been saved from a schism which has never yet been repaired, and which has wasted the national strength in barren contests. But Thiers and the rest of the Liberals wanted to have done with the elder branch of the Bourbons. They wanted to stamp out every vestige of Legitimacy. They wanted, as they said, to do for France what our own Whig aristocracy had done for England in 1688. They wanted to find a William III. After some hesitation, which is variously explained by the natural necessities of thought or the promptings of hypocrisy, Louis Philippe accepted the throne, which was offered by the Chamber of Deputies. It will ever be a serious question whether he should have allowed himself to be made more than lieutenant-governor of the kingdom, and the guardian of Henry V. According to one party, he had no right to let his conduct be guided by the debt of gratitude which he owed to Charles X. According to another, he had been actively intriguing for the possession of the throne, and his absorbing selfishness, which was the basis of his character, made him mistake the promptings of interest for the call of duty. But, at all events, if he erred, he met with a crushing punishment eighteen years later, when his own obstinacy provoked a revolution, and when he had to follow Charles X. into lifelong exile.

The Revolution of 1830 closed the second chapter in the career of Thiers, leaving him at the age of thirty-three among the most famous men in France. He might at once have entered the Cabinet, and indeed he was invited to become Minister of Finance a few months after the accession of Louis Philippe. "Are you ambitious, M. Thiers?" asked the king, as he proceeded to offer him that brilliant position. Of course Thiers was ambitious, so ambitious that, according to the gibes of his friends at Aix, he would be content with nothing short of a marriage with one of the king's daughters. But, as his very ambition taught him to be moderate, he declined to be minister until he should have gained further official experience. So he remained for a time in the position of what we should call Secretary of the Treasury. But the court could not afford to dispense with his brilliant qualities, and he became Minister of the Interior in 1832. He was then scarcely thirty-six years old.

I cannot pretend to sketch even in strokes of miniature his brilliant career as Minister of the Interior, Minister of Commerce, Minister of Foreign Affairs, and President of the Council. It is impossible to describe how he dealt with the insurrection in La Vendée, nor how he arrested its leader, the adventurous princess, the Duchesse de Berri, mother of the Comte de Chambord; how he encircled Paris with its great fortifications; how he completed such public monuments as the Arc de Triomphe, and the Madeleine; how he constructed canals and roads; how he had much to do with bringing the remains of Napoleon from St. Helena to Les Invalides; or how he nearly plunged France into a war with England on account of Mehemet Ali and the Eastern Question. I can only just allude to the brilliant and sometimes the reckless way in which he led the opposition to his great rival Guizot, during eight years' exclusion from power. I cannot stop to discuss even this last and greatest period of his life, when, chastened by age and the mighty calamities of a country which he passionately loved, he set himself to repair the ruin left by the Empire.

A few words, however, must be said about the general character of his home and his foreign policy. For a time after the Revolution of 1830, he profoundly disappointed his Liberal friends by his trust in the swift rude devices of military rule. Some of the laws for which he was responsible unpleasantly recall the acts of Charles X. In some degree the blame of the laws, if blame there be, must rest on his own domineering character. From his youth he had a passion for command, a determination to have his own way in the least as well as the greatest of things. A French wit satirised his craving for command, by saying that the ministry of 1840 was wholly made up of Thiers under different names. All his highly respectable colleagues were assumed to be mere clerks. Nay, Louis Philippe, the vainest and most self-sufficient of kings, sometimes found that he had a master as well as a minister. Thiers once flung down his portfolio in a pet, and darted out of the council chamber, because the king had dared to interfere with the details of some petty diplomatic arrangement, and for three whole days his colleagues could not prevail on him to come back. The same spirit was displayed under the Republic of 1848, Thiers lecturing and domineering all round. Even when age had mellowed his spirit, he would scarcely brook opposition in his own Cabinet. Yet such was the gaiety of his spirit, such the light and almost boyish vivacity of his tone, and such the real goodness of his heart, that people did not mind his intellectual tyranny. They laughed at it, and put up with it. That domineering spirit did at one period of his life, however, give him a dangerous liking for the devices of military rule.

But the truth is that, even if he had been as serene a constitutionalist as our own Sir Robert Peel, he could not have governed France with the quiet methods that do very well in England. In the days of Louis Philippe, the war of factions made it appear necessary for constitutional ministers to pass laws which in their hearts they must have condemned.

Thiers did much to increase the troubles of his own country by the chief literary devotion of his life. He did incalculable mischief by strengthening the idolatry of a man who has been the evil genius of France. Napoleon's consummate faculty for war blotted out half the good of the Revolution, by debauching the French people with a passion for military glory. His consummate faculty for despotism knit the already centralised institutions of France into a system which affords the most powerful lever ever fashioned for the hand of illegal violence. It is he more than any other person who has placed the French at the mercy of mobs and soldiers. The worship of Napoleon was comparatively feeble from the battle of Waterloo to the rise of the constitutional monarchy. He had left too many mourning homes, and the memory of too many disasters, to stir the pulses of his countrymen as he had done on the morrow of Jena and Austerlitz. But Thiers addressed a generation which had grown up since the Grand Army perished in the snows of Russia, and since Paris was occupied by the troops of the coalition. His own early training, his military tastes, his historical studies, all tended to make him find a hero in the great dictator, and the Napoleonic legend again grew beneath his hands. His history of the Revolution, and of the Consulate, and the Empire, revived the passionate admiration for the man who had shed the blood of his countrymen like water, who had extinguished their liberties, who had dwarfed their literature, and made France an intellectual desert, but who had given them a power and a glory which had made Paris think herself the heir of ancient Rome. It was fitting that Thiers should make his government bring back the ashes of Napoleon to the banks of the Seine. He acted like a devotee who should build a shrine for the relics of his patron saint. The revived worship of Napoleon has done incalculable injury to France. But for that new example of military force the Republic of 1848 might have withstood conspiracy, and France might have been saved from that second empire which began in crime and proceeded by steps of fate-like necessity to the capitulation of Sedan. Thiers was more responsible than any other man for the depraved ideals which made that empire a possibility. Indeed, it is a question whether he had not done at least as much evil as good down to that most illustrious season of all his life, when he set himself to retrieve a vast military disaster, when he refused to be a tool of dynastic selfishness, when he fought against that very imperialism which his eulogies had nursed, and risked everything to give France the priceless boon of a parliamentary republic.

One word must also be said about his foreign policy. It was closely connected with his idolatry of Napoleon, and it may be described as a passionate, blind, absorbing determination to sacrifice everything for the sake of French interests. The interests of other nations were of no account in comparison with the interests of France. If they stood in the way, they must disappear. Nay, they ought to disappear; for was not France the leader of civilisation, the most brilliant and cultivated of nations? Should not all other peoples copy the graces of her life? At all events, she must not allow her interests to be touched in any part of the world; and her interests were to be defined by the minister of the day.

She had interests in Spain, interests in

Italy, interests in Egypt, interests in Constantinople. Thiers calmly told Talleyrand that it was essential to the safety of France to keep the Spaniards under her control, and that every French government must put down every Spanish constitution, or, in other words, keep the Spanish people in subjection. On another occasion he defended in memorable terms that military expedition to Rome by which the temporal power of the Pope was re-established, and which was the final barrier to the unification of Italy.

But do not let us judge M. Thiers solely from the evidence of that explosion of cynical and shallow selfishness. It was after all a national feeling; it was called patriotism by the fanatics of French interests; and it met with a tremendous chastisement at Gravelotte and Sedan. The loss of Alsace and Lorraine, and the fine of two hundred millions sterling, are the price which France had to pay for the erection of French interests into the supreme law of national existence. That truth may have dawned on Thiers himself, on the evening of his long life.

It is a question whether Thiers was a great man or a great minister. But he was, at least, a typical Frenchman. Possibly he was, on the whole, the most really typical Frenchman of this century. Not that he had all the best qualities of his race. He lacked the profound passion which gives incomparable grandeur to some of the darkest as well as the brightest periods of French history. He lacked that blind faith in ideals which partially explains the political failures of his countrymen. He lacked that fanaticism which is as visible in the Reign of Terror and in every Parisian revolution as in the French wars of religion. He lacked that readiness to die for lost causes, that martyr spirit, in which the French people, with all their irreverence, are richer, perhaps, than any other nation. Thiers was not a good type of the more heroic qualities of his people. But heroic qualities are the gift of a happy or unhappy few. And Thiers did represent a great part of what is best in French character. He reflected, with marvellous vividness, the intellectual brightness, the vivacity, the ardour, the culture, the courage, of his countrymen; their cheerfulness under adversity; their faith in the great future which awaits France; their rich store of the social qualities which make her the most interesting of nations, and which light up the most sombre passages of her grand history.

CHAPTER VIII.

BONAPARTISTS.

It needed no bloodshed to pull down the Empire. The Empress and the courtiers knew that it was detested by the great mass of the Parisians, and that they could not rely on the army. The army of France always tends in the long run to be on the same side as the people, in spite of the military maxim that the first and last duty of a soldier is to obey the word of command. As for the officials and the courtiers, and the petted shopkeepers, and the speculators on the Bourse, who had been the mainstay of the Empire, the Government knew that it could not count on them. They vanished at the first touch of misfortune. And for some of them, in truth, France might not have been a very safe place after the disappearance of their protector. When the news of the capitulation of Sedan reached Paris in the evening, everyone knew that there would be a revolution next day. The only uncertainty was, what form it would take. Some Republicans imagined that it would be best to let the Empire finish the war which it had begun, to bear the ignominy and the chastisement of defeat, and then to overthrow it amid the indignation of the country. Some people, without being Bonapartists, would have preferred to have the Empire standing, provided the emperor himself should abdicate. But the clearer of the Republicans did not confuse themselves with nice calculations; they saw a bad government tottering and they struck it down. For good or evil, France must accept a democratic government. Hence she must elect between one of two systems — an Empire and a Republic. The chief strength of the Empire lies, no doubt, in the fame of the great man by whom it was founded. Vigorous attempts have recently been made to show that he is after all but a foul and misshapen idol. M. Lanfrey in particular has mercilessly stripped off the covering of romance which has been wrapped round the great conqueror. That Napoleon had no sense of honour, that he never scrupled to gain his ends by lying or treachery, that he was cruel, and that history presents no more striking example of selfishness—all this historians say and go far to prove. No doubt, also, he has lost his hold over the imaginations of the French workmen. They, at least, have learnt that the Republic has had no such deadly enemy as the great soldier who drowned the nation's memory of freedom in a flood of military glory. The Communists did no capricious act when they mischievously pulled down the Vendôme column. Heine, with the strangely prophetic sagacity of the poet, foretold that the mob of Paris would some day thus insult the memory of the emperor, and that they would complete their vandalism by flinging his ashes into the Seine. The first of the predictions has been fulfilled to the letter, the second may equally come to pass if Paris should fall into the hands of another Commune. Heine wrote before the *coup d'état* had overshadowed the glories of the First Empire with the guilt and ignominy of the Second. But the memory of the uncle now suffers for the sins and misfortunes of the nephew, and at this day no family is more bitterly hated by the Republicans than the Bonapartes. Nevertheless the name of the first Napoleon continues to fascinate a large part of the French people. In him the peasantry possess their only great personal memory. While Danton and Robespierre have bequeathed but vague memories, the "Little Corporal" has left vivid traditions in every cottage. Strangely enough, they forgave him although he took away their sons from the vineyard and the cornfield, and thus offended against the strongest passion of nature—their avarice. Some portion of the admiration springs, no doubt, from traditions left by those soldiers who came back to peasant homes after the glories of Jena and Austerlitz. Much of it is the remnant of a mistaken belief that it was Napoleon who broke the bonds of their feudalism, and assured to them the possession of their lands. Much of it is likewise rooted in the fancy that his government put down and kept down the mob of Paris, and all the other mobs which prevented the peasantry from making money. Such, at least, was the conviction which proved most serviceable to his nephew, after the Revolution of 1848 had frightened the class which cares more for its land than for any other thing in the world. Nothing did so much to reassure the peasants as the showers of grape with which the troops of Louis Napoleon shot down hundreds of innocent men, women, and children, on the boulevards; and the peasants were comforted rather than shocked by those mixed commissions which banished thousands of persons, equally innocent, to Cayenne. His ineffaceable crimes commended him to the ignorant vine-dressers. In his misdeeds, or at least in the strength of purpose and the freedom from scruple which they implied, a class of higher social station and more knowledge, found proof that the Empire was the best of all governments for France and for them. In return, the nation was to put its liberty into the hands of a military chief, who was widely supposed to be half a charlatan and half a knave.

The way to the Empire was smoothed, and, indeed, rendered possible by the Radical Republicans, when they made a change which they had believed would found the Republic on the adamant of the popular will. At last, it is true, the Republic has gained by the wild leap into universal suffrage. But at first that leap landed the nation in the lap of the Empire. Prince Louis Bonaparte and his little group of shrewd followers saw that the time was come for the establishment of an earthly providence compounded of ignorance, superstition, fear, vanity, and greed. They might have succeeded in the end, even if they had been less skilled in the art of the conspirator; for the country had but a small minority of convinced Republicans, and powerful classes were eager to settle down beneath the quietude of military rule. The Republic might no doubt have been saved by the National Assembly if the Legitimists, the Orleanists, and the Republicans had laid aside their animosities in order that they might work together, on the common ground of parliamentary rule. But it would have been about as hopeful to expect that a set of warring divines would lay aside their rival dogmas for the sake of their common Christianity. The Legitimist was more anxious to restore the elder branch of the Bourbons, the Orleanists to restore the younger, and the Republicans to buttress the Republic, than to act on the common ground of parliamentary government. In truth, the Legitimists cared little for parliamentary government, save in so far as it would help them to throw the ruling power into the hands of the lineally descended king. The Orleanists had not fully considered how it could be worked without the leverage of the middle class. For the moment, the Republicans equally put parliamentary rule in the second place, knowing that it would be established when the Republic should be secure. Thus all the parties intrigued against each other. M. Thiers, M. de Falloux, M. de Montalembert, M. Molé, M. Ledru Rollin, and M. Lamartine were all guilty of that error. It must be admitted that the several parties committed many blunders. It was extremely foolish of the Royalist majority, as I have already said, to lay a rude hand on universal suffrage, by imposing such conditions on the right of voting as to disfranchise several millions of people. Equally great was the error of refusing to increase the President's salary. The Assembly might have reflected that to keep such a man as Louis Napoleon short of money was more dangerous than to give him ample sums. The Republicans blundered most flagrantly by voting against the proposal to revise the constitution. But they also prevented the National Assembly from repealing the curious law which debarred the president from being re-elected. Such a prohibition, if it were to be enforced, would be a political death-blow to Louis Napoleon and his personal followers, because he and they had staked everything on the chances of his continuation in power. All the money that could be got by all the ways known to men of keen wits and small scruples, had been invested in the presidential election. Louis Napoleon and his little gang of followers were over head and ears in debt. The imperial ring therefore would be ruined if the National Assembly should not allow him to be re-elected, and they were made desperate by the refusal to amend the constitution. But the National Assembly committed the greatest of all its errors when, on the 17th of November, 1851, it rejected a motion for giving its own President authority to go directly to any of the military commanders, and demand such a force as he might deem needful to protect the Chamber.

The purpose of that motion was to guard the deputies against Louis Napoleon, who was notoriously eager to overthrow the constitution. But the Republicans feared that if the Royalists had any power over the army, it would be used to restore the monarchy. They feared the Legitimists and the Orleanists more than they dreaded even the conspirators of the Elysée. In union with the Bonapartists, they were able to defeat the motion, and thus, with the best intentions, they delivered the Republic into the hands of its deadly foe.

It is true that the National Assembly had not gone a step beyond its strict rights, that Louis Napoleon had not the faintest legal ground for complaint, that his accusations against the deputies were falsehoods, and that, in all probability, they would have repaired some of their errors if the life of the Chamber had not been cut short by violence. Universal suffrage might have been re-established, the President's pay increased, and the constitution revised. It is true, also, that the Assembly would have had good right to count on the fidelity of the President if he could have been bound by the most solemn of pledges and oaths.

But it remains true that the Republican party erred and was punished.

It is not very easy to anyone to speak about Louis Napoleon or his associates in a spirit of frankness, without seeming to repeat echoes from the slums of scandal. He was the ally of this country, and was believed to be the friend of England. He was held by many people to be the greatest statesman of a generation which has produced Bismarck and Cavour. Yet he and his personal followers and his party are viewed by a great part of the French people with a mingled hatred and contempt to which there are not many parallels in the records of political detestation. M. Gambetta, in one of his addresses, did not speak more bitterly than a vast number of Frenchmen feel when, after respectfully describing the Legitimists and the Orleanists, he came to the

Imperialists, and said of them he would not speak, because they were not a party but a horde. We must try and understand the causes of such a hatred. We must look, therefore, at the personal character of Napoleon and his associates, at the way in which they gained power, and the use to which they put it. All these facts are living forces at this moment.

Prince Louis Napoleon himself was an interesting man even before he became President of the Republic. His intellect, if very far from being first-rate, had the strength which comes from profound study of one great career. He had pored over the scriptures of the first Napoleon as devoutly as the old puritans nourished their souls on holy writ. His character had also gained an unusual power of waiting from long practice in the school of adversity. Nay, it sometimes profited by its curious mixture of definite aims and habitual irresolution. While he pressed towards the ends which he called his destiny, he hesitated from day to day and hour to hour as to the choice of instruments and opportunities. Usually it seemed impossible for him to make up his mind. Sometimes he gained a reputation for sagacity, because his indecision made him wait until the natural course of things did for him what he could not have done for himself. But, like many irresolute people, he would sometimes suddenly shut his eyes and rush to a decision; and then it was necessary for a Napoleon to speak with a Jove-like purpose. Nothing could be more Olympian in clean-cut peremptoriness of phrase than some of the decrees which were born of the travail of baffling changeableness. But he was chiefly distinguished because he had studied the art of conspiracy as laboriously as other men study the art of painting, or the practice of the law, or the theory of cuneiform inscriptions. He was as truly a plotter as Mazzini himself, without any of the disadvantages which came from Mazzini's highly-wrought moral sense. Like all born plotters, he had a positive liking for tortuous ways, even when the high-road lay clear before him. When he was emperor, and as absolute as any man can be in France, he did not deal frankly with his own ministers or diplomatic agents, but gave them varying instructions, so that the real lines of his policy should be hidden from all eyes save his own, and that he might intervene with providential decision and swiftness at the last moment. His policy with respect to the temporal power of the pope was a miracle of ambiguity. He gave one description of it in Rome, another in Vienna, a third in Paris, a fourth to anybody with whom he confidentially talked, and a fifth perhaps to the members of his own family. But it was not such a masterpiece of craft and success as the plot which bore fruit in the *coup d'état*. Even the victims of that conspiracy could not help admiring the minute attention which had been paid to its details, the foresight with which provision had been made for a multitude of dangers, and the skill which had been shown in the choice of the human instruments of treachery. The work was artistically complete. But Louis Bonaparte had more than one advantage, which considerably takes away from the intellectual merit of the deed. He was armed with a supreme want of scruple at those moments when the knot of a difficulty must be cut. He did not appear to see moral restraints when the fruits of a plot could not be reached by the artifices of the law. At such times he was capable of doing deeds of perfidy and blood, which offer perhaps the best grounds for believing that he was really a Bonaparte by race as well as by name. At critical moments he had, therefore, an immense advantage over honest men. Very soon after he became President he began to undermine the Republic, and then he brought into play his power over the art of the conspirator, and his freedom from the prejudices of the moral law. He threw his temptations far and wide. He tried to catch the commander-in-chief, General Changarnier, with a golden bait; but, although that soldier was as fond of power as Louis Napoleon himself, and a good deal more vain, he had a considerable share of the professional honour which is no bad substitute for a moral sense, and he was also as fastidious in the choice of his companions as in the fashion of his dress. Louis Napoleon was more fortunate in his attentions to lesser people. "*Si nous faisons les généraux*," he is said to have carelessly observed to his man of all work, Fleury, and straightway the lax moral school of Algeria was ransacked for soldiers who might be trusted to shoot down any rash defenders of the law. The search was eminently successful. Louis Napoleon also tampered with the common soldiers and with petty officials. And his whisperings, his promptings, and the open treachery of his agents, were no secret to his political opponents. It was perfectly well known that he was trying to overthrow the Republic. His doings were freely canvassed in the lobbies of the National Assembly, and they were made the subject of menacing hints even in the speeches from the tribune. Colonel Charras, one of the Republican leaders, slept with loaded pistols by his bedside, because he anticipated that the agents of the Elysée would try to seize him and the other prominent deputies. He was one of the few Republicans who voted for the proposal to give the President of the National Assembly the power of calling for the protection of an armed force; M. Grévy, the present President of the Republic, was another; and it is amazing that these eminent men were not followed by their colleagues at a time when the rumours of a coming *coup d'état* were among the commonplaces of the street. Perhaps Republican enthusiasm made it difficult for the members of the Left to believe that the head of the State could be guilty of such perfidy as he was about to commit.

But even Louis Bonaparte's readiness to tell a lie and shoot down innocent people would have been unavailing, if he had not been aided by an admirable band of friends; and it ought to be admitted that he drew them to him by the influence of his good qualities. It is of course a vulgar error to suppose that a man may not be a charming companion because he has done some deeds of superlative wickedness. There is a grim story that "*dans la vie privée, M. Robespierre était un homme fort aimable;*" and it is an interesting psychological fact that Tropmann murdered five persons to provide for his poor relations. Louis Napoleon, who was neither a Robespierre nor a Tropmann, was in many ways a very amiable person. M. Emile Ollivier, in the address which the Academy would not allow him to deliver, said that, when he came to know Napoleon III., his regard for him deepened into affection. Although a renegade would naturally magnify the idol for which he had left his old gods, there is no reason to doubt the sincerity of a tribute which might be matched by compliments to all the equivocal characters of history. Louis Bonaparte deserved to be liked: he was an agreeable host, an indulgent friend, and a kind master. There must have been real goodness of heart in a man whose followers clung to him through the worst as well as the best of his fortunes, and who forgave them even when they dipped their hands into his purse by shorter ways than those of waste. Attempts have doubtless been made to lessen the merit of their fidelity. Some of them, it has been said, were of such a moral hue that they could have found employment in no party with a character to lose; and others, even when living in exile, may have shrewdly guessed that the constitutional monarchy would lead to the Empire, and thus to a paradise of adventurers. When he reached the throne, they clung to him of course, because his fall would cast them adrift on a world which has only a limited need for men like M. de Persigny. Such suppositions may explain why particular men were faithful to the emperor, and why others worked for the restoration of his dynasty. But it is nevertheless true that he was a kindly chief, that he had a long memory for personal services, and that he had the heart of making his attendants like as well as serve him. He was never unscrupulous except when he had a purpose to serve. Thus, during his exile in England and his tenure of the presidency, he gathered round him a band of devoted and admirable followers. There was, for example, M. de Maupas, who, as his President of Police, did much credit to his powers of selection. It was M. de Maupas who had to arrest the most dangerous members of the National Assembly, and the safety of the plot greatly depended on him. He did the work very neatly indeed, and he has lived to reap the fruits of his skill. At the late general election, when a coalition of Orleanists and Bonapartists tried to strangle the Republic, he had the courage to become an official candidate, and he had the honour of receiving support from the government of the Duc de Broglie, whose father he put in prison for defending the law. Persigny was a real believer in the gospel of Bonapartism. To him it was a kind of religion, and it paid for his devotion by brushing away his poverty and making him a duke. The imperial gold which he put into his pockets was as good as other gold; it bore the mark of the mint. The dukedom was not quite so good as some other dukedoms; it bore the mark of the Empire. General Fleury, another of the conspirators, did good work in a smaller way than Persigny or Maupas. Louis Napoleon found him a bold adventurer, who knew the points of a horse, and could profit by them, who had seen Parisian life, and, being innocent of political restraints, could admirably fetch and carry for the chief conspirators. It is sometimes said that he played a small part in the night of the *coup d'état*; but his friends give some reason for believing that statement to be a calumny. They rebut it, telling a curious and well-known story. Louis Bonaparte, they say, showed signs of flinching at the last moment, after he had risked his own life and the lives of his associates by distributing the proclamations, in which he announced that the Assembly was dissolved and that the president had made himself a dictator. It was Colonel Fleury who, at that critical moment, took out a pistol and dared him to draw back. So, at least, say Fleury's friends, and there is no sufficient reason why he should be robbed of that distinction. There is no less reason because the boldness which he then displayed in a back room of the Elysée seems to be the only military distinction that he gained during the Napoleonic reign. He won his promotion in the drawing-room of the Tuileries, and he is still a general. Saint Arnaud was made of different stuff. He was a bright clever man, who could wield a sparkling pen and play on the fiddle. His freedom from scruples had brought him into collision with the scruples of the law. But he was, nevertheless, a bold dashing soldier. There are men, whose whole life is a preparation of some masterpiece of evil; and Algerian warfare, as practised by Saint Arnaud, was no bad apprenticeship for the service which began with the shooting of innocent Parisians on the boulevards. But the most important of all the conspirators, the very brain and nerve of the plot, was Louis Napoleon's illegitimate half-brother, Morny. He was in many ways a very interesting character, and he had long been admired or feared by a certain class of the higher society in Paris. His life had been enlivened by what is called "intrigue," and he had earned a good deal of condemnation, but no contempt. His whole career was striking, for he was a personage whose clear and hard brain would have made him distinguished even if he had been an honest man; whose finished politeness and self-control were rooted in a contempt for mankind; whose cold, insatiable, artistic appetite for pleasure has made him a profitable theme of study to the writers of fiction; who never allowed the rushes of the Decalogue or even of the criminal law to stop the short cuts to fortune open to the cool and the bold; who practically disdained the fastidious maxims which forbid a minister to play on the gambling-table of the Bourse, with the loaded dice of early information; and who did not escape the imputation of having helped to push France into the Mexican War at the bidding of pecuniary motives. There was nothing commonplace about the illegitimate son of Queen Hortense. As Minister of the Interior, he managed the *coup d'état* with a coolness, a freedom from scruple, a skill, and a success, which drew words of reluctant admiration even from his victims. Had he been less careless of praise, he might have urged that it was he, rather than his brother, who ought to receive the chief praise for the deeds done on the 2nd of December; and we may admit that had he been as responsible as Louis Napoleon, he would have been as infamous. He was, at least, the genius of the Second Empire. Morny was, in fact, a self-contained, cultivated, polite, agreeable, clever, perfectly finished blackguard.

Such are specimens of the men who enabled Prince Louis Bonaparte to destroy the Republic. It will be seen that they were not a very reputable set. That fact, indeed, was the sting of the *coup d'état*. Constitutions have been overturned and oaths broken before 1851. France had been ruled by fanatics and ruffians, as well as by respectable and great men. But never before had she fallen into the hands of adventurers, who treated her as a mine, out of which they were to dig their fortunes. For the first time, the country which thought itself the most brilliant in the world, and which could never forget its grand history, was to be *exploité,* France was to be ruled by men some of whom the better sort of people would decline to meet at dinner. But Napoleon III., as he came to be styled, soon found that it was no light thing to hurt the self-respect of the most sensitive society in Europe. Although as anxious as the first emperor had been to draw the historic families to the Tuileries, he could not persuade them to come. They "cut" the Emperor and the Empire too. One of the greatest of them, when asked why he never went to the Tuileries, said that his coachman could never find the way. They laughed at his Napoleonic airs, and always spoke of him as "*celui-ci.*" Hence, he had to fill his reception-rooms with the men who represented the wealth and the adventurous spirit, rather than the rank or the culture of Paris. He was equally slighted by another class which is of more lasting importance in France. As the Augustus of the Empire, he wished to be the patron of art and letters, and he gathered round him some artists and literary men. The artists were among the best of their kind, for art has no politics. But the men of letters were not quite so emblematic of France. Peculiar reasons, it is true, made a writer of such brilliant talents as Merimée a domesticated pet of the Tuileries, and he correctly styled himself "*fou de l'Impératrice*" when sending that lady the manuscript of a very clever and not very decent story. The author of "Mademoiselle de Maupin" also found the Empire a suitable kind of government. Some of the dramatists earned its decorations by epigrammatically hinting that the first duty of power was to make things pleasant; and for a time Edmond About lent his bright pen to the better part of its policy. But these were exceptions.

Most of the best writers disdainfully held aloof from a government which was splashed with the blood of the *coup d'état,* and from the adventurers who had taken the France of Molière and Voltaire into their keeping. Nothing hurt Napoleon III. more grievously than the scorn of the literary class, for his own instincts were almost as literary as they were political. He had a literary rather than a political way of looking at public affairs. The merit of his state papers lay in the phrases, the allusions, the form of the expression—in a word, the literary qualities rather than the ideas. He had published some little books, containing thoughtful sentences, and a passable imitation of good writing. He had composed part of a big book on Cæsar, which, although a dull specimen of historical literature, and an immense indiscretion, was not commonplace. Such labours were supposed to denote a keen ambition to find a seat among the forty of the French Academy. But he never had a chance of getting into good society at the Palais Mazarin. He would have given much for the power to turn the delicate scorn of such pens as Prévost Paradol's into the sweetness of flattery. But it was not to be. Play as he might at being Augustus, he could not find his Horace, and from time to time such books as "Les Châtiments" warned him, in Chateaubriand's phrase, that Tacitus was already born into the empire. "*Si vous arrêtez Victor Hugo,*" Morny is reported to have written, during the reign of the *coup d'état*, "*faites en ce que vous voulez.*" But in giving that order Morny made a mistake. At all hazards, he ought to have got rid of the man who could, and who clearly would, weave round Morny's handiwork a legend that would live as long as France.

Napoleon III. had to bear a slight of still more moment to the head of a new empire than the disdain of patrician families and men of letters, and that was the refusal of the most eminent statesmen to become his ministers. He was keenly anxious to secure their services, even on the morrow of the *coup d'état*. But throughout his reign Thiers, Guizot, the De Broglies, and all the old parliamentary chiefs scornfully made known that they would not become the associates of M. de Morny and M. de Persigny. They declined to support a system which had been built on perjury, and which was killing the better qualities of the nation. So long as Morny lived, the Empire could count on the guidance of unflinching shrewdness, and occasionally it enlisted a very able man of business like M. Rouher; but usually it had to give office to men who could be little more than clerks. They might have done passably well if watched by a free parliament, and spurred on by a high sense of duty; but, as the Corps Législatif and the Senate were filled by creatures of the Empire, the flatteries of those bodies were usually more dangerous than open assaults. They hid the thinness of the crust which separated the Empire from the nether fires. Still more perilous was the tone of the court itself. Since it had been reared by crime for the most vulgar of personal ends, and since it was cut off from all the nobler public spirits, it could be guided by no higher motive than that of self-preservation. The courtiers assumed that power and splendour were things to be enjoyed while they lasted. It is said that the more thoughtful of the revellers did not expect to have a long lease of the Tuileries. But they were not the first sybarites who had said: "Let us eat, drink, and be merry, for to-morrow we die." The wild gaieties of the court throw some light on the amazing decline of political morality among the servants of the Empire. The instincts of self-preservation will not work out the way of safety for dynasties whose officials are athirst for pleasure, and have ceased to believe in any higher duty than obedience to the word of command. In time, many of them will not take the trouble to give that word, and many more will not obey it. They will amuse themselves and pay themselves. They will not take care of a dynasty which has ceased to take care of itself. Public honour has a better right than chivalry to be called the cheap defence of nations, as the Empire was to find when the first impulses had spent their force, and its more intrepid spirits had passed away. The moral laxity of the court had spread even to a service on which a despotism is expected to pour out the riches of its skill. There could be no more bitter satire on the fancied excellence of despotism than the state of that army which Napoleon III. had pampered. The carelessness and incompetence of the commanders, the peculation, the laxity of drill, the ignorance of the officers, and the general negligence of duty, were such that he organised failure for twenty years. The result was written out at Sedan.

Louis Napoleon's chief aim was to be the earthly providence of his subjects; to be the Cæsar of the modern Rome; to give the patricians honours, wealth, glittering gewgaws; to please the plebeians with shows, largesses, the glory of conquest, and the vanity of triumph. All these devices were borrowed from the vulgarest tricks of the Roman emperors, and of their imitator, the first Napoleon. The immediate reward was the praise of the large and varied class which sought for a millennium of material prosperity. Nowhere is that class larger than in the country which, at the summit, is the most brilliantly intellectual in Europe. No literature contains more allusions to the pleasures of money-making than the literature of modern France. The novels of Balzac, which are steeped in the atmosphere of the Bourse, and add thrift to the list of the Beatitudes, merely exaggerate a profound instinct of French existence. The first Napoleon might have styled his own countrymen, much more truly than ours, a nation of shopkeepers. No country at least has so strongly developed the talent for saving, or so nearly erected it into a moral law. The Empire, as I have already said, delighted the peasants, who were too ignorant to care for anything beyond

s

their fields, and who fancied that it possessed the secret of disarming the terrible Socialists of Paris. It gave more positive because more comprehensible delight to the gamblers in the Bourse; they shrewdly saw that a Napoleon could not afford to govern like a humdrum Louis Philippe, but that he must strike the imagination of his subjects by brilliant surprises, which could not be found in peace. The speculators of Europe would vote for war every year to increase the stakes, and they would clamour for any Barabbas, who would help to keep Europe in a ferment. The Empire found other allies among the shopkeepers, to whom the making of money is the end of life, and whose sordid ideas are softened neither by such political enthusiasm as that of Parisian working-men, nor by such religious instincts as those of our own lower middle class. It delighted the rich, vulgar, pushing, soulless people, who scarcely know what is meant by nobleness, to whom religion means something to be said out of a book, and who look upon the "lower orders" as a species of beings who must be put under the care of the Minister of War. It seemed almost an ideal government to the idle frivolous men and women, to whom life without a gay court and an infinite round of frivolity is not life at all. They were promised stillness in the revolutionary faubourgs, and endless gaieties, subsidised by the Minister of Finance. But the Empire was welcomed most heartily by those soldiers who assume that the nation lives for the sake of the army, and who are as eager to gain distinction by the slaughter of their fellow-beings as astronomers are to discover a new planet, or philanthropists to reclaim a fever-den. The barrack-room is seldom a good school of politics. A military training tends to hide the wondrous play of those moral forces which keep society in equipoise. In France they have been more obscured than in any civilised country. The army was pleased therefore to know that the nation should henceforth be ruled by the word of command. It felt sure that the potent syllables of the drill-ground could bring quiet, and it did not see the difference between quiet and peace. An overheated steam-engine is never more quiet than when the safety-valve is screwed down. The device of the military statesmen, when they heard any noise, was to give another turn to the screw. They were also delighted by the military airs of the Empire. It was pleasant to think that the army was no longer to be governed by talking barristers, but by its own chiefs and in its own way. The emperor loved to pose as a soldier, and the youngest of the sous-lieutenants sometimes felt themselves to be of more account at the Tuileries than great civilians. The army instinctively felt that, as it had raised the government to power, the government must flatter it, and pamper it, and cut out work for it, to prevent it from going over to the Orleanists or to the Republicans. It dimly knew in advance that there would be Crimean wars, and wars for an idea, and wars for the payment of Jecker bonds. A Pretorian Guard is the same in all ages of the world. Let the throne of the Cæsars be put up to sale, and the auctions will be frequent and the prices high.

The Empire was very much admired in England, and Napoleon III. himself was heartily welcomed when he came to visit the queen for the purpose of getting into the good society of his fellow-sovereigns. Partly, the homage was paid to the ally of the Crimean War; partly it was the result of the good-will which he was supposed to feel for England, and of the admiration with which he was believed to regard some of her institutions. It was also a tribute to the success with which he was thought to be governing what was held to be the most intractable race in Europe. If free Englishmen were reminded that he was a despot, they were ready with an answer, that a despotism was good enough for the French. There remained a large share of genuine admiration for the firm hand with which the Empire kept down all high-flown aspirations towards progress. Vulgarity, social prejudice, and the passion for dominion were in favour of imperialism in England as well as in France. All parties which fancied political enthusiasm to be dangerous, and which felt that high ideals were troublesome to the arrangements of an old society, saw a friend in Louis Napoleon. Could the success have been final, it would have cast a blight over the Liberal instincts of half Europe; it would have been like the iceberg which chills the temperature of the encompassing sea.

Still, the Empire could not have lasted for nineteen years, without the aid of some higher qualities than frivolity, force, and greed; and in truth it had some positive merits of considerable value. Most of them sprang from the character of the emperor himself. He was not only an amiable man when he had no personal enemy to crush or sinister object to gain, but he had room in his mind for some large plans of statesmanship. Long study in prison and exile, and long brooding over the grandiose conceptions of the first Napoleon, had given him ideas which might be called "viewey," but which were certainly not commonplace. He displayed a good deal of moral courage as well as mental clearness in driving the reluctant French towards the ways of free trade, by means of the Commercial Treaty with England. If it be said, that it would have been better to have left the fiscal tariff full of wasteful absurdities than to have brought it more nearly into agreement with good sense by means of sheer force, I have nothing to reply. Still, despotic authority could not have been employed in a better way. The wish to be the Cobden and the Peel of France may have been an imitation of the first Napoleon's ambition, to go down to posterity with the Code in his hand; but, in any case, it was a more worthy desire than to play at being the hero of Marengo, and to this day it gives some measure of respectability and strength to the imperialist party. Nor could any merely commonplace mind have seen how inevitable and overmastering had become the tendency of like nationalities to group themselves under the same government. That tendency springs partly from the spread of knowledge, which has shown those scattered parts of a possible unity that they have a common history, common likings, and ideals, and interests—all the subtle and mysterious stock of kindred qualities which are the basis of family life. It springs, too, from the vast change which our time has seen in the art of war. The destructive force of its weapons has been multiplied tenfold, and the cost of them has grown in proportion. Thus the change has added to the power of the greater and richer states, because they can most easily bear the expense of the new system. At the same time a network of railways and telegraphs has enabled a fatal blow to be struck at any government, with a swiftness which would have seemed incredible half a century ago.

The campaign of 1870 has shown that a few days may decide the fate of a great country. But the condition of success is that gigantic armies shall be held in leash, and thus all the chief powers have engaged in a ruinous attempt to outstrip each other in military equipments. Hence, the smaller states were never so overshadowed and menaced as they are to-day. They all seem fated to disappear, unless general exhaustion or some other change in the art of war should stop the present rivalry. Masses of people have always an instinctive sense of coming danger, and such divided nationalities as Italy and Germany felt that they must group themselves under one head to escape from lasting subjection to some alien power, or from a weakness which is a first step to decline and fall. The rise and tide of nationalities has already swept away the sandbanks which were raised by the Congress of Vienna, and it will continue the work of destruction until the peoples of Europe shall be grouped according to those natural divisions which are dictated by mutual sympathy and community of interest. It is, perhaps, no credit to the heir of Napoleon that he should have been quick to see the force of a tendency which was to destroy the artificial fabric built by diplomacy on the ruins of the Empire. He had noticed that, in modern Europe as in old Rome, the mob might be made the best ally of despotism, and hence that plébiscites might do more for him than campaigns. Perhaps his fatalistic ideas helped to show him that if the growing determination of nationalities to group themselves together was the master current of the time, he would shatter his power by trying to stem the stream. There is a philosophical fatalism which cuts clean through the devices of diplomacy. Such may have been the reason which made him look on listlessly and helplessly while the German people were making gigantic steps towards unity, and while many of the ablest Frenchmen were saying that he must strike in or perish. Nor is it difficult to understand why he should have helped to make Italy into a nation. In that country he had spent the happiest years of his youth, and he seems to have had something like a generous sympathy for its people. Among his early dreams had been the vision of a liberated Italy, and he had taken part in plots against the foreign power to which it was then subjected. He had been a member of the Carbonari in those mooning days, and he had fought against the Austrians. It is quite true that he would not give a thought to Italy when he had to choose between her welfare and his own power. That fact had been made clear by the compact with the Clerical party, and the expedition to Rome. But when Piedmont began to take steps for the deliverance of Italy; when Orsini tried to shoot the emperor, in the belief that the emperor stood in the way of her freedom; when Orsini's last letters gave the imperial Carbonari clear warning that his life would never be safe until he should have kept his early oath by striking a blow for Italy; and when Pietri, the Prefect of Police, warned him that the threat was not empty—then Louis Napoleon launched his army against Austria. He allowed himself to be stopped halfway by the menaces of Prussia and the fears of troubles at home. It is true that he shabbily paid himself for the blood of Magenta and Solferino with the fee of Savoy and Nice. It is true that he would never allow the nation to occupy Rome. Still, we may admit that he would have done more for Italy if he had been less afraid of the Clerical party, and that the campaign of Piedmont is the best act of his reign. It is the only one of his acts which has stirred the praises of generous souls; and it is no light thing to have won the plaudits of Mrs. Barrett Browning.

Less might have been said in praise of the campaign in Italy if it had not been assailed by the chiefs of the constitutional party. But it is a melancholy fact that they, the old Parliamentarians, who ought to have given France lessons in Liberalism, were on this occasion less Liberal than their enemy. Practically, they were on the side of the smaller Italian governments, and therefore on the side of tyranny. Nothing did so much to make the Empire seem respectable as the aid which it gave to the rising nationality of Italy at a time when M. Guizot, M. Thiers, and such of their younger followers as M. Prévost-Paradol, were helping the attempt of all the reactionaries of Europe, and those of England among others, to stop the great popular movement. "Such," it was sneeringly said, "is French Liberalism!" In truth the real Liberals of France, who were mostly Republicans, were more heartily in favour of a united Italy than the emperor himself. The old constitutionalists were misled, partly by their fatal alliance with political Catholicism, and partly by their inveterate belief in the power of "management." Some of them wanted to support the Papacy for reasons bound up with the very existence of the Clerical faction; and all of them fancied that, if the smaller States of Italy were to be destroyed, the whole of Europe would slip away from the control of statesmen. The foundation of European order was, they said, the great international treaties, and especially the contracts framed by the Congress of Vienna. Those arrangements were the constitution of Europe, and the devices through which its affairs could be "managed" by a small family party of able men. Take away those treaties, and Europe, they declared, would be at the mercy of military and popular forces, just as France was when a reckless mob pulled down the monarchy of Louis Philippe. The Italian States rested, it was said, on treaties which formed part of what was grandly called the public law of Europe. It might be true enough that the King of Naples, the Duke of Modena, and even the Pope himself ruled badly; but after all they were independent sovereigns, and hence they had as much right to be left alone as any King of France. Make good the principle that one State might invade another, in defiance of treaties, and on the plea that he intended to stop misrule, and Russia, it was said, might claim a right to invade Turkey; for surely the

Pope, and even the King of Naples, did not govern their small States so badly as the Sultan governed his huge empire. That reasoning was urged with great ability by the present Duc de Broglie in a book which was prophetic. The very plea on which Piedmont and France overthrew the old system of Italy was employed by Russia when she went to help the Bulgarians. The campaign in Italy gave the inheritors and the patrons of misrule throughout the world notice to quit. It was a precedent of incalculable importance. But the constitutional statesmen who put their trust in the "public law" of fleeting, fragile, preposterous treaties were living in the fools' paradise of their own pedantry; and Napoleon III. helped to bring Europe back to the rude realities of fact when he asserted that the living wishes of a nation were of more account than the dead parchments of Congresses, which may be as far distant from possibility as if they had been held in the moon. "Public law" will become somewhat more than a fine phrase when the forecasts of diplomacy are more modestly brief, and when nations are intelligent enough to dictate at first-hand their own foreign policy.

On the other hand, the very aid which the Empire gave to the movement of nationalities hastened the inevitable day of its own ruin, for the Nemesis came with a united Germany. And the way in which the Empire slipped down to ruin was terribly instructive. Not very long before its downfall it might have seemed to a superficial glance firmer than ever; but that appearance was deceptive. In spite of gaudy public shows, foreign alliances, and boisterous foreign policy, diplomatic triumphs, victorious campaigns, and appeals to the spirit of Chauvinism by the master of demagogic phraseology at the head of the State, the clouds of popular discontent grew and gathered. The peasantry were becoming less frightened by Socialistic nightmares, and less pliable; the higher classes and the men of culture held aloof as disdainfully as ever from the adventurers of the Tuileries; and the Opposition

—that Opposition which could once "have all gone home in a cab"—grew every year more threatening. It had already a master spirit in M. Gambetta. The Empire found that it could neither suppress nor cajole that Republican and Democratic party which was capable of carrying into politics a religious enthusiasm; which had never forgotten, and never would forget, the traditions and glories of the Revolution; and which hated military rule, because the political methods of the barrack-room are insulting to the sense of personal dignity. That was the party which held Paris and the other great towns in its grasp. That was the party which kept Napoleon III. in chronic insecurity. It ridiculed and worried him. Its very "chaff" was a serious annoyance to a government largely dependent on vanity. "*On siffle; voilà l'empereur!*" Its diatribes, its lampoons, its agitation, and, more than all, its silent hate, so weakened his government that, throughout his reign, he had to give spurts of nervous vigour to its enfeebled frame by the stimulants of plébiscites and wars.

Wars were a necessity. They could not all be successful when the whole of Europe was arming to the teeth, and every nation was casting about for allies. But the tenure of the imperial power depended upon unbroken success. The first great defeat would bring it to ruin; and if it had not been engulfed at Sedan, it would have found a grave elsewhere.

CHAPTER IX.

THE BONAPARTISTS.

In the latter days of his power, Napoleon made a desperate effort to regain his lost authority by trying to convert himself into a Corsican edition of Louis Philippe. The edifice of liberty was at last to be crowned; France was to be free; the heir of the great conqueror and the hero of the *coup d'état* was to become a kind of constitutional king. Prince Napoleon—a real Bonaparte in mental faculty as in blood, but also a Jacobin in political and religious ideas— had been steadily saying that the government of his cousin must thus transform itself or perish. Some of the Royalists and of the younger constitutionalists were so far satisfied with the change as to accept office. M. Emile Ollivier, the son of a Republican, who had been proscribed after the *coup d'état*, and himself a leader of the Opposition, became Prime Minister; Count Daru and M. Buffet joined the Cabinet; and to the astonishment of everybody, M. Prévost-Paradol laid down the pen with which he had chastised the Empire, in order to put on its diplomatic livery, and go as its minister to the United States. A flutter of excitement passed over the more credulous parts of Europe, and the Whigs of England sent their compliments to their new brother. But the emperor felt that, before sinking into the position of a Louis Philippe, he must fortify himself with another plébiscite. So he submitted the constitutional changes and the merits of the dynasty to the judgment of the populace. M. Buffet and Count Daru would not remain in the Cabinet of a sovereign who thus showed an unalterable attachment to one of the first devices of the Empire. M. Ollivier was more complacent. Meanwhile, the peasants were solemnly told that they must give this last mark of their confidence in the emperor, in order that he might maintain peace at home and abroad. The plébiscite was peace. The secret reports of the prefects, which were published after the fall of the Napoleonic dynasty, show that the peasantry were deeply anxious to be saved from the stimulants and the cost of what is called "glory." But the emperor was familiarising his brooding, hesitating mind with the idea that he must fight the great military power which was rising beyond the Rhine. He might have longer resisted the temptation if he had been the man he once was, for seeing that the chief political force was the unifying current of nationalities, he must have known that to attack Prussia, the head of a unified Germany, was to venture on by far the most perilous enterprise of his reign. He had missed the chance of striking Prussia in 1866, when she was fighting Austria. Not merely Bonapartists, but Orleanists and Republicans, I fear, got into the habit of saying that the glory of France would be effaced if Prussia were allowed to remain the first military power of the Continent. But his health was sadly shattered, and his power of will had been impaired by the disease of which he ultimately died.

Meanwhile the Empire had lost the gilding of its better days and its reputation for luck. It had never recovered from the disasters of the amazingly foolish expedition which the army made to Mexico, at the prompting of M. de Morny's avarice and the Clerical passion for power, to gather the bad debts of M. Jecker and to found a Catholic empire by the side of the great Protestant republic. When the Mexicans not only baffled the army of France by setting up their old republic, but shot that Emperor Maximilian who had crossed the sea under the flag of France; when his poor wife, after frantically beseeching his protector to send him help, was driven raving mad by the consequences of the refusal; when it was whispered about that the French troops had been turned homewards partly by the fear of Prussia, and partly by the threats of the great republic which had crushed the slave-holding confederacy; it was impossible to put a blind of lies between the eyes of the nation and the loss of imperial renown. It began to be said that Mexico was the Moscow of the Third Empire. Still greater was the mischief done to the dynasty by the results of the war between Prussia and Austria in 1866. The emperor, it was said, had been culpably neutral when the German Confederation, by attacking Denmark, had begun the military greatness of Prussia; and had he not been infatuated, it was added, he would have poured an army into the Rhine provinces when Prussia began the campaign which ended in Sadowa. Thus he might have won back the provinces which were added to France by the first Napoleon, and torn from her after Waterloo. Nay, Prince Bismarck, in the course of his frank talks with his Boswell, Dr. Busch, has admitted that Prussia could not have hindered France from thus advancing her frontiers. Calm students of the national history may be allowed to doubt whether such an invasion would have done any good to the Empire in the long run; but it is only fair to say that, in the opinion of so able a witness as M. Prévost Paradol, such a triumph would have established the Napoleonic dynasty. But the emperor had not the same decision as the statesman who was welding Germany together with blood and iron. He hesitated until the opportunity was lost. Sadowa had been fought and won before the French envoy, M. de Benedetti, could reach Prince Bismarck; and then France was mocked with assurances that she might take Belgium if she liked, but warned that every foot of German territory would be defended with all the strength of the new nation. Napoleon III. was too late. He was Louis the Unready. Let it be said to his credit, however,

that his hesitation partly came from his fitful
respect for the rights of nationalities. So much
is made clear by his dealings with the Prussian
ambassador at Paris, Von Goltz. M. Thiers
would have taken the side of Austria at the
outset from a cynical disdain for all other rights
than those of France. The emperor himself
quickly put aside his religion of nationalities
when he saw how formidable Prussia had become.
Indeed his refusal to let the Italians get Rome
for their capital—the fatal "*jamais*" of M. Rouher
—showed how lightly he held the tenets of his
political religion when they came into conflict
with the interests of his dynasty. There can
be no doubt that he began to familiarise his
dreamy brooding mind with the idea that a war
with the new military power was inevitable. It
was believed to be inevitable even by men who
did not wish to bring it about—by such men
as M. Prévost Paradol, who said that the two
nations were like two trains which, placed on
the same line of rails, and propelled from

opposite ends of the line, must come into collision midway. A war of revenge was demanded by the Chauvinists, whose passion for conquest had been stimulated by M. Thiers, himself, in his glorification of the First Empire. What France had to revenge, the Chauvinists would have been puzzled to say. They were content to sum up their creed in the axiom that France must be the first of military nations. Prussia had no right to come in the way of her divine right to bully her neighbours. More thoughtful politicians urged that a powerful Prussia would be as aggressive as France herself had been; that she would lay her hand on Holland and become a great maritime power; that she would give a protecting hand to Italy, and cancel the *"jamais"* of M. Rouher with an edict of militant Protestantism.

The speculators on the Bourse, if we may trust M. Thiers, spoke in favour of war when the opportunity came with the cynicism of pecuniary gain. Thinking that the war of 1866 had now lessened the trust in the continuance of peace, and that trade was consequently suffering, they urged that the Empire should make a short and sharp war to regain its supremacy and increase the dividends of France. Dealers in the funds are among the worst judges of political events in the world, because they look mostly to the chances of the morrow, and they would lose their capacity for their work if they were to cultivate philosophical breadth of view. So they thought that a campaign of six weeks would suffice to rectify the accounts of Prussia and France. It is said that some of the very highest of them were so ignorant of the capacities of the two nations, as to hold that opinion. *"C'est un mauvais moment à passer, quelque cinquante mille hommes à sacrifier, après quoi l'horizon sera éclairci, et les affaires reprendront."* Such is the reading of their judgment given by M. Thiers.

It is not improbable, however, that the emperor might have withstood such promptings. He must have guessed, even if he did not exactly know, that his army was weaker than his ministers dared to confess. He must have known that the war with Mexico had terribly drained its strength. Perhaps, also, he suspected that the army had suffered from the system of *virements,* or the practice of secretly taking money which the Chamber had voted for one purpose and devoting it to another, which the ministers dared not avow, but which the peculiarities of the emperor none the less made a necessity for the moment. Perhaps he suspected that the strength of regiments had been cut down, and the supply of artillery pinched, in order to provide funds for uses more closely akin to the daily life of the court. Although the most indolent of despots—although his dislike to hard work formed a fatal contrast to the habits of men like Peter the Great, Frederick the Great, his own uncle, and the other men who had guided military States—he may, perhaps, have glanced at the despatches in which Colonel Stoffel, the military attaché at the court of Berlin, and

M. de Benedetti, his ambassador at the same court, had explained the real strength of the Prussian army. His own soldiers had certainly not taken so much trouble; they were the most dangerous set of luxurious and ignorant triflers that ever thronged the antechambers of a military prince. The emperor must also have been held back by his real perception of the strongest political currents of our time.

But far stronger than the prompting either of the Bourse, or the Chauvinists, or the ignorant soldiery, was that of the two parties to whom he owed his throne.

Firmer, because more besotted, minds than his own were urging that the dynasty could not be founded without the aid of another victorious war, and that this time the foe must be Prussia. If he could win back the Rhenish provinces, which were conquered by his uncle, and wrested from France by the Congress of Vienna, the glory of the achievement would be such, that he might laugh at the criticism of M. Thiers, the sarcasms of the salons, and the lampoons of M. Rochefort. Sooner or later, it was urged, France must fight Prussia; one or other must be supreme. Prussia, it was said, knew the necessity so well, that she was arming to the teeth; and the only question for a practical Frenchman was whether she or France should strike first. In reality, a practical Frenchman, even if he had listened to that profoundly deceptive argument, would have waited until he should be certain that his country was ready for battle. No doubt, that is what the emperor would have done if he had followed his own opinions, for his habitual shrinking from any great decision would have been fortified by some knowledge of the real military strength possessed by Prussia—a knowledge of which the military and ecclesiastical butterflies of his court were absolutely ignorant. But he was flung into the abyss of war by the two forces to which he owed his throne—the dynastic and the Clerical parties. Vengeance had come at last in the shape which had at first clothed victory. The plébiscite brought to light the alarming fact, not merely that a large minority of the people would not have the Empire on any terms, but that it had been denounced by more than fifty thousand voices in the army and the navy. When Cæsar learns that about one in six of his legionaries is sullenly looking out for his successor, he naturally feels that it is time to offer the distraction of distant war. A faction of sincere bigots and sceptical traders were equally of that opinion. They had a strong garrison in the Tuileries, and the leader of it was the Empress. They instinctively and justly felt that their fine schemes of papal and sacerdotal power would be shattered if they did not stop the growth of the great Protestant State, which had reared itself in the centre of Europe. There remained those friends of the dynasty, those families of the Tuileries, those members of the family itself to whom the existence of the Empire was the first of necessities. A pretext for combat was readily found in the candidature of the Prince of Hohenzollern for the throne of Spain; and it must be confessed that Count Bismarck took no pains to avert the struggle. He rather did everything in his power to push France into the abyss. He probably thought, that as the challenge would come sooner or later, it was better to pick up the glove at a time when Germany was ready and France was not. But the Chauvinists of the sacristy and the barrack-room seemed to be foiled for a moment by the prudence of the King of Prussia, who allowed the candidature of his kinsman to be withdrawn. One day M. Ollivier confidently said in the lobbies that peace had been assured, and on the same day the Duc de Grammont, the Minister of Foreign Affairs, had written a short address which was intended to tell the Corps Législatif that the honour of France had been satisfied. But in the evening, at St. Cloud, the manuscript of this little bit of imperialist self-glorification

THE BONAPARTISTS. 289

was discussed at a council, representing the family as well as the Ministry, and it was altered to a form of fatal menace. The half-Clerical, half-military dynastic party thought that it could not afford to throw away the chance of a war with Prussia. Now or never could a deadly blow be struck at the rising Protestant power. Now or never was the opportunity of making the reversion of the throne to the young Prince Imperial secure. So the ministerial address was altered into an insolent statement that the King of Prussia must pledge himself not to allow his cousin to renew his candidature, and that France would exact the fulfilment of her demand. Such a claim, when made with such insolence, was intended, of course, to make war inevitable. Everybody knew what it meant. The Republicans and the old constitutionalists saw in it the most wanton of provocations.

M. Gambetta and M. Jules Favre desperately strove to stop the fatal course of the Ministry;

U

and M. Thiers uttered a prophetic warning. "*L'histoire, la France, le monde,*" he said, "*vous regardent. De la décision que vous allez prendre dépendent la vie de milliers d'hommes et, peut-être, les destinées de notre pays.*" But the creatures of the Empire drowned the protests of the best men of France; a hired mob in the streets shouted "*À Berlin!*" the boudoirs of St. Cloud and the sacristies of the capital were in a flutter of triumph; M. Ollivier accepted the responsibility of the war with "*un cœur léger;*" and, in short, religion, the Empire, and the dynasty were saved. Some people took credit to themselves for having given France the last little push down the inclined plane of salvation. "*Cette guerre, c'est ma guerre à moi; il me la faut.*" Such are the words put into the mouth of the empress, and her flatterers do not seem to have been instructed to give them a denial. The emperor himself was less cheerful, and he complained to an Englishman of congenial temper that France had slipped out of his hand. That falsehood was dictated by a prophetic sense of the terrible indictment which lay in the near future. Nor was he kept long in suspense. A coming crowd of tremendous disasters told of the ruin which nineteen years of imperialism had brought to the splendid army of an older France. The valour of the common soldiers might have probably retrieved even the blunders of the commanders but for the dynastic necessity of the Empire. After the loss of Wörth and Gravelotte the emperor himself telegraphed to Paris: "*Tout peut encore se réparer.*" There was one last chance, and that was to withdraw the remaining army towards Paris, so as to prevent the investment of the capital. When Mont Valérien and its companions were crowned with guns it had been intended that, in case of a siege, a great force should operate within the circle of the forts. Such had been the purpose of M. Thiers. Had that been done the result of the war might still, no doubt, have been adverse, but Paris could not have been easily besieged, and France would have been able to exact far better terms. And the step which prudence urged might have been taken so late as the September of 1870. A large and unbroken army lay encamped at Châlons, between Germany and Paris. Its commander, Marshal MacMahon, knew that he ought to fall back upon the capital; Prince Napoleon passionately urged his cousin, the emperor, who was with the troops, to obey that plain dictate of safety; and that counsel was supported even by M. Rouher, who had come to the camp. But the empress and Palikao frantically telegraphed that the return of a defeated emperor would give the signal for a revolution, in which the dynasty might be overthrown and his own life sacrificed. The Pretorian Guards were ready to abandon Cæsar. The emperor listened to that counsel instead of resolving that his dynasty should perish rather than his country, and Marshal MacMahon was weak enough to let his own judgment be overborne by the dictates of the imperial family. Hence it was determined that he should proceed towards the northern frontier, with the view of doubling the German army and joining Bazaine. The march, it is said, was made in the face of a despatch from Bazaine, which rendered it in the highest degree improbable that the two forces could meet. It was made towards a point of the Belgian frontier at which less than the genius of Moltke and a smaller army than his would have sufficed to hem them within a semicircular band of artillery, and leave them only the alternative of surrender or a march into Belgian territory and a capitulation. For dynastic reasons, Napoleon marched straight towards the trap of Sedan. Nemesis had come at last; and modern history contains no such other instance of tremendous chastisement.

Nor is it possible to spare much pity for the fallen greatness of the man who had been the dictator of Europe. His case was very different from that of Charles X. or Louis Philippe. Charles X. was led astray by an inherited fanaticism which did not lack a touch of dignity, and which had no taint of criminality. Louis Philippe, if not free from the stain of meanness, had on the whole been a good king. But Napoleon III., in spite of much personal amiability, of some statesmanlike aims, and of considerable ability, had debauched the mind of France for twenty years by perjury, disdain for the sanctity of the law, massacre, despotism, a frivolous court, reliance on a besotted bigotry, wars made at the dictate of national vanity, and finally by a war intended to give strength to his dynasty. No government of recent generations so systematically poisoned the wells of the national life. However terrible may have been the losses of Gravelotte, the capitulation of Sedan, the blood which dyed the battle-fields of the Loire, the capture of Metz, the siege and fall of Paris, the greatest pecuniary fine ever exacted, and the surrender of two provinces, still, even at such a price, France was cheaply rid of the Empire. Unless we keep these facts in view, we cannot do justice to the passionate hatred with which Louis Napoleon and his dynasty are regarded by the best class of Frenchmen. Thus alone can we explain the cause of the Republic.

My friend intended to have expanded these notes—for, brilliant as many of them are, they are only notes—into a bird's-eye history of France since 1815, and especially to have added a sketch of the Republicans and their fortunes since 1870. This, as I judge from long and frequent conversations with him, would have been the most important and the most effective portion of his work. Probably no man not a Frenchman watched France so closely. Thoroughly familiar with her modern history, and acquainted with most of her eminent men, Mr. Macdonell had a sympathy with French Republicans, a comprehension of their motives, their objects, and their foibles, which gave him often an insight into their fortunes that looked to less instructed men like prevision. During the whole of the long struggle, which began with M. Thiers's appointment at Bordeaux, and ended with M. Grévy's election in February, 1878, he never doubted that if France were consulted, the people would decide as a body for the Republic. In advance of almost all Englishmen he discerned that the French peasantry, hating Legitimacy, which they still associated with feudal oppression, and disenchanted with Bonapartism, were willing, if only property were made secure, to trust the Republic; and that with the severe suppression of the Commune their fears for their property had disappeared. He never, therefore, through the whole of the contest lost heart, or dreaded anything for the Republic, except an appeal to force, which at the same time he felt confident the condition of opinion in the army would not allow to be made. When in 1873 the resignation of M. Thiers was accepted, and Marshal MacMahon was elected to prepare the way for monarchy, Mr. Macdonell asked which monarchy the Monarchists intended their agent to select. When, in June, 1871, the Assembly, on the motion of M. Casimir Perier, formally recognised the Republic, he said that henceforward the conservative feeling of the peasantry, or rather their reverence for legality, would be on that side; and when, in 1878, the Marshal President, convinced that France was with him, appealed to the people against the Republic, he maintained steadily that the reactionaries had blundered, and that the only chance of suspending the Republic, even for a time, lay in a *coup d'état*. Only once was his confidence momentarily shaken. Thoroughly as he understood France, he never quite understood the restraints which bind the leaders of her army, the reluctance to risk a civil war "in the barracks;" and when the decision of the electors was known, he for a few hours expected a resort to force and a military *coup d'état*. The opportunity passed, Marshal MacMahon resigned, M. Grévy, the most determined of Republican

x

statesmen, was elected President, and Mr. Macdonell declared the Republic finally established. There might, he said repeatedly, be any number of dictatorships during special crises, but for centuries no throne would be set up again in France. The conflicts of the future would not be between the Republicans and Monarchists, but between the Church and the Voltaireans; the one conflict in which he thought the Liberals, being false to their principles, and fighting persecutors with persecution, might be repeatedly, though for short periods, defeated.

The conflict between the Republicans and the Anarchists he did not dread at all, and in fact did not believe in. It was, he constantly asserted, a British and not a French idea of the facts. "The French are essentially the most conservative people in Europe, the people most keen for acquisition, and the people among whom property is most widely diffused. Taking the landholders, the rentiers, and the people with hoards together, eight Frenchmen in every ten hold property, and they are perfectly certain not to give it up. They are not generous, they never subscribe, and they always push all claims to money to their precise legal limit. They will never consent to any system of division, or to any annexation of inheritances by the State; and the Communists of the cities, if they rise a hundred times over, will be put down a hundred times. Society in France is founded on a rock. It is the one country in Europe in which social revolution, that is successful revolution, not a mere émeute, is impossible. The Church is the one Republican danger, or rather the Republican inability to leave the Church alone." This was in fact the central idea of his total judgment of France. Let her but be Republican, be organised in accordance with the instincts of her people, and civilisation has nothing to fear from France. The social revolution may come, but it will not come thence. The Republic therefore, he believed, would succeed, and ought, as the form of government likely to endure, to enjoy the sympathies of all Englishmen who wish France to be contented and at rest. It was from this standpoint that these notes were written, a standpoint from which argument the most pertinacious or most brilliant never moved James Macdonell.

M. TOWNSEND.

THE END.

CHARLES DICKENS AND EVANS, CRYSTAL PALACE PRESS.

www.ingramcontent.com/pod-product-compliance
Lightning Source LLC
Chambersburg PA
CBHW022102230426
43672CB00008B/1258